HOW YOU CAN USE THE
TECHNIQUE OF CREATIVE IMAGINATION

HOW YOU CAN USE THE TECHNIQUE OF CREATIVE IMAGINATION

Roy Eugene Davis

CSA PRESS, *Publishers*
Lakemont, Georgia 30552

*To you
who are involved with
the process of discovery.
I behold
you unfolding all possibilities.*

PUBLISHER'S NOTE TO THIS EDITION

How You Can Use the Technique of Creative Imagination has a remarkable publishing history. Over forty printings of two prior U.S. editions have been distributed, and it has been published and widely circulated in the German, Italian and Portuguese languages in Europe and South America. It has also been featured on many radio and television shows.

It is the publisher's dream that this newly written and expanded edition will serve equally well in the years to come.

ABOUT THE AUTHOR

Roy Eugene Davis began his spiritual training in 1950 after meeting his guru, Paramahansa Yogananda, in Los Angeles, California. Mr. Davis is the spiritual director of Center for Spiritual Awareness, the author of many books which have been published in several languages, and a world-traveled speaker and teacher.

Programs have been offered in major U.S. cities, Canada, Japan, Brazil, England, European cities and West Africa. Regular meditation seminars and retreats are offered at Center for Spiritual Awareness world headquarters, located at Lakemont, Georgia, in a quiet setting amidst the wooded mountains of northeast Georgia.

Foreword

Sooner or later, in this sphere or another, every person will come to terms with the universe and learn to consciously relate to and function in it. I am not so inexperienced that I expect every reader of this book to immediately grasp the total import, solve all personal problems and fully actualize inborn capacities. I know that for most it will require patient study and practice to master states of consciousness and explore all possibilities. Here are the master keys for one to use, to begin where you are and continue in the direction of the fulfillment of all worthy purposes.

Let it be understood from the outset that you should not become involved with these procedures with the idea of becoming rich in the world's goods and soon able to dominate your environment. Prosperity there will be, and ability to influence, but always in harmony with individual soul destiny and the freedom of others to express their own righteous inclinations. The immature philosophical conclusion that you "can be what you want to be, do what you want to do, and have what you want to have" cannot result in useful ends. One who plunges into life with this attitude is certain to eventually experience a rude awakening—when he discovers that it is not egocentric passion which results in true happiness, but conscious cooperation with the laws of nature which uphold orderly completion of purposes.

The dedicated person must be willing to learn, to undergo needed transformation and to apply himself with all diligence. In the emerging New Era there is already too much evidence of people making the mistake of assuming that with a little learning irresponsible behavior can then follow. I emphasize that you must be open to discovery and committed to the application of these principles. Only in this way can there be orderly unfoldment, increased proficiency, emotional maturity and final fulfillment.

Much of what you read here will not be new to you, but knowing *about* something is not the same as *knowing*. When we know, and when we are responsive, we can use what we know to positive advantage. Often the principles are almost clearly understood, yet we are not able to use what is known because the nervous system must be trained and we have to acquire experience by becoming involved in the process of living. Through the right use of creative imagination, and personal involvement with worthwhile projects and relationships, you will acquire all the training you need as the result of experience. You will become healthier, more mentally competent, more emotionally stable, and more spiritually aware. Your brain and nervous system will become adapted to processing higher states of consciousness. As a result your appreciation for living in the universe will be enhanced.

From childhood I have known how to enter into imaginative states, envision desired ends and have them unfold into manifestation. Even during early years, while still experimenting with the process, I realized the necessity for self-responsibility and for avoiding possible interference with the life plans of others. After some years of rigorous study and training as a young adult, I followed my dreams, the inner urge to unfold and express, and discovered that almost unlimited possibilities lie before one who is sufficiently aware and courageous enough to explore them. What

I share in this book is what I have found to be true, and it will be supported by the testimony of countless others who have also learned to use these principles.

The field of unlimited possibilities is within you, at the deepest level of your being. At this level you are one with the vast, pure field of consciousness out of which all nature has emerged and by which it is nourished. All you need, or could want, is already available to you. We live in a universe of constant change and inexhaustible resources. What will you do now that you know these things? What awaits you as you enter into the inner space of imagination and begin to expand awareness so as to comprehend all things and be the person you are destined to be?

I know for certain that you will never be the same again. Had you not known these things you could have, perhaps, been excused. But now you know them, and from this day forward you will walk in the light of understanding.

— *Roy Eugene Davis*

February 4, 1988
Lakemont, Georgia

Contents

technique *(n.)* 1. Procedure used to accomplish purposes. 2. specialized performance of such a procedure.

creative *(adj.)* 1. Having the ability or power of creation. 2. original, productive.

imagination *(n.)* 1. Forming of mental images or concepts of what is not present to the senses. 2. the faculty of doing so. 3. the ability to reproduce images stored in memory or of recombining former images of former experiences in the creation of new images different from any previously known. 4. the product of imaging.

Wisdom is the principal thing; therefore get wisdom: and with all thy getting, get understanding.

— *The Proverbs 4:7*

Seek ye first the kingdom of God, and his righteousness; and all these things shall be added unto you.

— *The Gospel According to Saint Matthew 6:33*

I have often thought that the best way to define a man's character would be to seek out the particular mental or moral attitudes in which, when it came upon him, he felt himself most deeply and intensely active and alive. At such times there is a voice inside which speaks and says, "This is the real me."

— *William James*

Man may attract and direct any force in the universe by making himself a fit receptacle for it, establishing a connection with it, and arranging conditions so that its nature compels it to flow through him.

— *Ancient axiom*

CHAPTER ONE
Use Possibility-Thinking and Creative Imagination to Enter into a Conscious Relationship with the Universe

The innate urge of every person is to consciously have a personal relationship with the universe and to move freely through it. We can experience such a relationship and flow easily through space and time because we are designed to do so.

Why is this so, and how can we know it? It is so because we are spiritual beings and the universe is a responsive organism, in which we live. We can know it through study, disciplined practice and personal experience. We can take on faith the words of more conscious people and, by entering into the process of living with faith, prove to ourselves the principles they teach us. You are not asked to blindly believe what is here shared. You are only encouraged to accept that which feels right to you, in your heart, and test it in the arena of daily life.

Life is precious to all creatures, and every living thing desires to be secure and nourished, and to fulfill intended purposes. Man, too, desires these things, and more; because of his inborn capacity to extend awareness beyond the boundary of self-consciousness, man desires to expand his awareness to embrace divinity. Man alone, because of his unique status and refined nervous system, has the capacity to become cosmic conscious and to enter into a purposeful relationship with the universe.

In using the term "cosmic conscious," I am referring to our ability to become increasingly aware of the nature of the universe in which we live, its origins and the principles underlying all phenomena. Scientists of today are more and more sounding like the seers of old, as they share their conclusions about the characteristics of the universe. The basic understanding is that all of the forces of nature are but variations of a single force, and that nature is but a play of cosmic forces. All occurrences in nature are unfolding in a field referred to as Universal Mind. It is the primal substance of which all forms are made, and beside it there is nothing.

As specialized expressions of pure consciousness, we exist in this field of Mind Substance, expressing through our personalized mind (which is a fragment of Universal Mind) and our physical body (which is comprised of the ingredients of nature). Therefore, by successfully adjusting our states of consciousness or levels of awareness, and by intelligently using our mental capacities, it is possible for us to live freely in an open universe. That is, we can live without restrictions and flow with the current of evolution which carries creation along.

The Need for Spiritual Awakening and Intelligent Use of Inborn Capacities

If it is true that we are designed to function freely, why do not more people do so? There are two basic reasons: 1) lack of spiritual awareness, and 2) incorrect use of inborn capacities. If one is spiritually aware it will be easy to use abilities and, if one is only partially spiritually aware, the correct use of abilities will result in increased spiritual awareness.

So although I write about function and mobility I am not suggesting the use of available abilities for purely materialistic ends. I am stressing the ideal of conscious, purposeful living in order to satisfy basic needs and to fulfill destiny. It is possible for one to learn to satisfy needs and live a reasonably secure life, but this is not the final purpose for our being in this world. A birth and a physical death are but transition phases in the soul's longer sojourn, so it would be folly to think merely in terms of being reasonably successful during the few decades allotted to us now on Planet Earth.

Only you, after much prayer, self-examination and contemplation, can determine your personal destiny and what is really important for you now and in the future. Therefore, do not err in thinking that we are here examining ways to satisfy immature whims or shallow desires. Worthy dreams can unfold as circumstances in our lives, as we progress in understanding and skill, but these are seen as fleeting events when the larger picture is known.

There is a benevolent Power nourishing the universe, and we can learn to cooperate with It. Be wary of any personal urge to use the Power; rather, be more open to the possibility of the Power using you for Its purposes. In this way you will never make any major mistakes and you will not injure yourself, or another.

Do not think that you will ever be the master of your fate, the sole controlling influence of your destiny—for you will not. It is possible, however, and even desirable, that you learn to be a willing participant in life's journey and that you learn to make wise choices and use your abilities creatively and in harmony with natural law.

Many people, when self-centered, use their creative abilities unwisely and, as a result, cause problems for themselves and interfere with the harmony of nature. Some, with noble intentions, try too hard to bring about "useful" changes and later find, to their dismay, that they were not as effective as they assumed themselves to be.

Much testimony abounds as evidence that many creative and so-called "successful" people are not fulfilled inwardly, and that their laudable efforts, viewed from a more expansive vantage point, have barely made a useful difference in their understanding or in the circumstances of the human race.

Think reverently about the matter. Come to some inner understanding about your purposes in life. Think about whether or not what you do, or plan to do, is really worthwhile and if it will make a difference. It will be worthwhile if you go deeply enough into your real nature; then what you experience and do will make a decided difference in your spiritual awareness, and in what is accomplished through you.

Do not be afraid to enter into a relationship with life. It is for this reason that you were born. You are not here to remain withdrawn or passive, nor are you here to blindly grasp at the world. You, and everyone else, are here to become increasingly conscious, to learn how the universe works, and to play your unique role in the unfolding drama. As you do this you will learn to relate to the objective world, the outer realm, while you remain grounded in the subjective, the inner realm which supports the outer.

By examining only the outer surface of nature we fail to comprehend the inner workings which make possible the outer. So true spiritual growth results in an increasing appreciation for what occurs in the realm of nature as well as an understanding of inner processes. In this way we are able to understand the metaphysics of creation, the higher laws which determine occurrences at the level of matter.

Possibility-Thinking as
a Way to Expand Awareness

It is so easy for us to become complacent and bound to our restricted patterns of thinking, believing and behavior. Thankfully, there are things we can do to remove awareness from self-imposed limitations. One of the more useful procedures we can use is that of intentional possibility-thinking. It is really very easy to do, and it requires but a gentle exercise of imagination.

Whenever you feel inclined let your imagination explore new, different and interesting possibilities—for yourself, for your involvement with your world, and for others. When you become aware of mental, emotional, physical or environmental limitations, imagine how it would be to be mentally free and creative, emotionally balanced and mature, physically vital and functional, and free to move through the world without any barriers or limitations. In this way you will be able to experience, in imagination, unlimited possibilities. Creative ideas will begin to flow, solutions to problems will surface in your mind, inner serenity and peace will be experienced, vital forces will surge through the body, and the world will appear to you brighter and replete with opportunities.

You see, if we have become caught in the snare of limited thinking, feeling and behavior, it is often difficult to envision alternative circumstances. But when we engage in possibility-thinking we are able to liberate ourselves, at least temporarily, and explore larger dimensions.

It is an axiom, a statement considered to be fact, that

whatever we can inwardly envision as possible can outwardly express as conditions and circumstances. Whatever we can believe to be true, if it is in harmony with natural law (subtle and material), we can experience.

Can you believe for yourself spiritual awareness, mental creativity, emotional maturity, physical vitality, harmonious relationships, and success in all useful ventures? If you can, your worthy dreams can manifest in your world.

Many who consider themselves to be on the spiritual path, involved in practices designed to lead to enlightenment, are reluctant to set goals or desire even worthwhile change in their lives because they are afraid of further binding themselves to the wheel of causation. Or they may mistakenly believe that even intelligent goal-setting is evidence of being materialistic and self-serving. This is not so, for one who *correctly* uses his innate abilities is merely fulfilling useful purposes. Intelligent use of abilities does not bind us; instead, such activity can liberate us from all bondage.

To set worthwhile goals and to desire useful results need not be done from a consciousness of lack, during which we mistakenly assume that the realization of our dream will add to our sense of beingness. Instead, the ideal is to function from the awareness of being whole and complete now, so that our creative involvements are natural and orderly expressions of our inclination to experience freedom in the world while, at the same time, we render useful service. In this way accomplishment of our goals is not a reward, but merely something which unfolds as a result of intelligent function. We then continue to express with benefit to society and nature, and when the time comes for us to depart from this world we do so easily and without looking back.

As a result of daily exercising imagination, through

possibility-thinking, soul capacities are awakened and expanded to the extent that we find it easy and natural to be aware of a universe that to us is increasingly without boundaries.

From time to time, when you are alone and quiet, write down your aspirations, your hopes and dreams—to clarify your thinking and focus your attention. In this way you will learn to regulate mental states and avoid fantasy and useless daydreaming.

Remember Who You Are, and
Remain Aware of Life's Purposes

The purpose of creation can be known by observing the workings of nature. Is it not true that nature moves ceaselessly in the direction of growth, needed transformation, and completion? Because you are involved with nature you, too, are moving ceaselessly in the direction of growth, needed transformation, and completion. So do not think that possibility-thinking, the exercise of creative imagination, and the unfolding of other abilities you have are for the purpose of manipulating your private world in a selfish, immature fashion. To the contrary, with increased understanding and the capacity to exercise available skills, comes also the need to be honest and sincerely responsible. Therefore, as we become more conscious and more able, we should also attend to the cultivation of the virtues, so that all that we do is the highest and best of which we are capable. Even extraordinary ability, if not tempered with purity of motive, will not prove useful for long.

The time will come, as the result of patient practice and increased awareness, when you will seldom need to consciously engage in possibility-thinking, for you will always be aware of the totality of life. Then your thoughts, your words, your actions, your mere intent, will be in perfect alignment with the purpose of creation. Seeming miracles will occur, the unfoldment of subtle causes, but you will not be conscious of causing them. You will be so established in goodness that virtue will flow out of you, and around you, as naturally as you breathe the air which serves your body. You will discover that living is effortless because the mighty current of life finds no resistance in you.

1. You are designed to flow easily through space and time.

2. Your awareness can expand to embrace divinity.

3. You are a specialized unit of pure consciousness, expressing in a field of Mind Substance.

4. There is a benevolent Power nourishing the universe and you can learn to cooperate with It.

5. Do not be afraid to enter into a creative relationship with life. It is for this reason you were born.

6. Whatever you can envision as possible, in harmony with natural law, can express outwardly as circumstances and experiences.

PRACTICAL APPLICATIONS

Use the exercises and procedures recommended after each chapter to become familiar with the principles and practices taught in this book. As you do this you will become aware of useful changes in attitude, feeling and behavior. Be as self-honest as you can and as self-responsible as you know you should be. You may prefer to read the book completely and then read it again, using each chapter as a lesson to be more carefully studied and applied. Should you decide to work your way through the book, giving attention to the practical application sections as you study each chapter, this would also be a helpful procedure.

1. *Read this book when relaxed and in solitude.* Settle down and be completely open to learning. If you like, meditate or contemplate for a few minutes beforehand, to calm the mind and be more receptive. Along with information you will acquire insight and perceive the real meaning behind the words.

2. *Experience the Usefulness of Intentional Affirmations.*
To affirm is to declare a thing to be so. Constructive, intentional affirmations enable us to adjust states of consciousness, attitudes and feelings in constructive ways. When using an affirmation always speak in the *now*. For instance:

> *I am calm, clear, open and receptive to learning and to actualizing what I learn. I am self-honest and self-responsible for my life. I am open to all good as I flow through the universe with perfect faith.*

Repeat this affirmation *aloud*, in firm, clear tones, three or four times. Repeat three or four times more *quietly*. Repeat three or four more times in a *whisper*. Repeat a few times *mentally*. *Rest* in the silence for a few minutes, *feeling* the truth of what has been affirmed.

NOTES

Lord, make me to know mine end, and the measure of my days, what it is, that I may know how frail I am.
— *Book of Psalms 39:4*

And be renewed in the spirit of your mind; And. . .put on the new man, which after God is created in righteousness and holiness.
— *The Epistle of Paul the Apostle to the Ephesians 4:23, 24*

Are you in earnest? Seize this very minute;
What you can do, or dream you can, begin it;
Boldness has genius, power and magic in it.
Only engage and then the mind grows heated;
Begin, and then the work will be completed.
— *Johann Wolfgang von Goethe*

The Great Void cannot but consist of ch'i (life essence); this cannot but condense to form all things; and these things cannot but be dispersed so as to form (once more) the Great Void.
— *Chang Tsai / Chinese philosopher*

CHAPTER TWO
Remove All Barriers

Look upon living in this world as a great adventure. Consider yourself to be a hero-spirit, a righteous and fearless being, able to master yourself and to understand the laws of nature. The material universe is but the outer expression of finer forces and principles, and this can be understood by any reasonably intelligent person.

Our desires and needs, and our degree of understanding, determine our sphere of action. We are in this world now because this is where we can best express at the moment. Those who have no need for this world have already left it; the fact that we are here is evidence of purposeful involvement. What you do with your life now will determine your future tomorrows, in this and other spheres.

Use the recommendations and planning procedures that are included in this book in order to enter fully into a conscious relationship with the process of living. Do not merely read these words, and then pass your time in idleness. Knowledge without experience is impotent.

I once visited the offices of a hugely successful book distributor. I was shown through the offices and warehouse and marveled at the efficiency of the procedures. I was shown the mail room, the telephone room, and also the machines which were used to record incoming orders during the night hours when the offices were closed. The business manager told me, "You see, we have removed every obstacle for the customer. Our communication lines are always open."

Are your personal communication lines open? Do you think without confusion, function without conflict and perceive your world without error? If you do not, there are things you can do to remove all obstacles, all barriers— barriers which may be preventing successful conclusions to your creative efforts.

While there may be external obstacles—and we will examine a few possible ones—the major restrictions are within us, due to less than optimum awareness and the conditionings which may be present in the mind, the emotional nature, or the body itself.

One who is intent upon learning how to live victoriously must learn to live the *inner way*, and not overly struggle with circumstances and conditions in the environment which, after all, are for the most part the effect of human causation. While there are certain environmental circumstances which are caused by natural forces, these can be adapted to, and often modified. Most of our experiences, however, upon honest evaluation will prove to be the result of our own states of consciousness, our mental states, and our behavior.

Imbued with purpose, set short-term and long-term goals. This will give direction to your life, and the achievement of short-term goals will build confidence, increase your experience, and prove to be invaluable as a learning process. Even if you make a few minor mistakes in judgment, at least you will have had experience, and you will learn how to avoid similar mistakes in the future.

Success is Natural;
Failure is Due to Error

Success can be defined as "the favorable result of endeavors and efforts." A person is successful when he is living a life worthy of him and experiencing the completion of worthwhile purposes.

Include in your personal success program the ideal of fulfillment on all levels—spiritual, mental, emotional, physical, in relationships with others, and in worthy projects. If you ignore one or more levels you will not be a whole person. You will not be fulfilled. You will not be truly happy or truly prosperous.

Do not shrink from the idea of being prosperous. To *prosper* is "to thrive, to flourish, to be successful in all worthy pursuits." Nature, as is readily apparent, prospers. We, too, should prosper in all ways. Remember, it is not enough for us to be somewhat spiritually aware but lacking in other areas of our lives. It is not enough to be mentally creative but lacking in spiritual awareness. It is not enough to be physically healthy but materialistic in outlook. Therefore, include in your personal program *all* levels of fulfilled living.

If one is not successful there exist errors in judgment, perception, or behavior—perhaps in all three. We can learn to use our intelligence, to see clearly and discern without error, and to perform our duties with perfect poise and skill, *if* we are willing to extend ourselves, awaken and use the inborn capacities of the soul.

Recognize and Dissolve
Self-Defeating "Myths"

A *self-defeating myth* is a sustained belief which is not based on fact. Until we are completely clear and possessed of understanding we often entertain false beliefs, such as, "I'm a born loser. . .No one could ever love me. . .It's impossible to be free in a world dominated by greedy people . . .It's not "spiritual" to prosper. . .My problems are due to past karma. . .My horoscope is afflicted. . .The only way to succeed in this world is to take advantage of the system (or others). . .My problems are inherited and there's nothing I can do about them. . .I'm not smart enough to accomplish anything. . .I'm a slave to my addictions. . .God is an imaginary character. . .All men (or women) are selfish. . ." The list is limited only to the speculation of the individual.

No matter what mistakes you may have made in the past, no matter what others have done to you, or said to you, no matter what your experiences have been and how you have been affected by them, you can emerge from all pain and confusion and learn to live as a clear, conscious and functional person.

I know something about you. I know that behind the facade of your personality, behind the conditionings of your mind, behind the senses of your body, you are a perfect, complete and fully competent being. I know this about you because this is true about every person on the face of the earth. We are all spiritual beings, specialized units of pure consciousness, and any other seeming condition is but due to wrong perceptions, wrong beliefs, and conditionings.

The first step in the direction of freedom is to clearly understand, and accept, the fact that you are a spiritual being, expressing through a mind and a body. The next step is to purposely begin to take charge of your thinking habits and your feelings. All that then remains is to clear restricting conditionings and circumstances and become involved with meaningful pursuits—and you can do it.

What is true for you is determined by your present state of consciousness (your level of awareness) and your mental states. Really, all healing, of any kind, occurs when we experience a clearing of our mind and consciousness. When the inner causes of outer effects are dissolved, external limitations can no longer remain.

Have you come to terms with your past? Very few people have. Most people have painful memories hidden in the recesses of the unconscious, memories they prefer not to recall. And along with those painful memories much vital force is suppressed, vital force which would be more productively utilized in creative endeavors.

Isn't it true that when you review your past, back to earliest memories of childhood, some remembered incidents cause involuntary emotional reactions? The times when you were hurt, misunderstood, incorrectly counseled or instructed, when you failed, when you were rejected or neglected, or when circumstances denied you freedom and self-respect—these incidents have left their scars, and they surely have altered your view of the world.

The past cannot be changed, but your feelings and attitudes about past incidents can be changed. You need not remain a victim of anything that has occurred in your past.

A major step in the process of clearing traumas relating to past experiences is to decide, right now, to be a mature, responsible person and to never again blame any other person or any incident for your present attitudes, feelings or circumstances.

We've all known people who constantly blame others for their personal failings. Society is heavily populated with such self-styled "victims." We see them in jails and prisons, on the streets begging, in the mainstream coping, and at every level of the socio-economic strata complaining. We see among the halt, the lame, and the spiritually blind many people who could, if they only would, make decided changes in their lives and accomplish many worthwhile things. They have only to renounce their self-defeating routines and, beginning where they are, unfold their capacities and explore the almost endless variety of opportunities which life is even now presenting to them.

I know from experience how it is to grow up amidst circumstances which can result in adverse mental conditioning. I remember the post-depression years, the uncertainty of war time, the general belief among the people of the rural midwest that life was a matter of hard work, "making do," getting by, and being thankful for whatever you happened to have, and I know people who have never recovered from the effects of their youthful conditionings. I also know many people who were made of sterner stuff, who were able to see through the self-defeating myths almost cherished by many people in their childhood communities. I've seen the emotionally deprived remain deprived, and I've seen those with self-esteem and a higher vision move free from the past and soar to the heights of personal achievement.

What is it that makes the difference? Is it that circumstances determine? Is it that only people of genius excel? Is it that destiny plays trivial games with human beings? No, *what makes the difference is individual awareness, perception, maturity, choice, and behavior.*

Every rational person has freedom of choice. No one can dictate to another what that person can think, believe and imagine. Please understand that you have freedom of choice to determine your states of consciousness, your mental outlook, your emotional condition, and your behavior—and according to the choices you make, you will experience exactly what you are in consciousness, in believing, and in performance.

Your state of consciousness is determined by what you feel and know about yourself. If your feeling-knowing is that you are a weak, inept person, this is what you will reveal to the world. If your feeling-knowing is that you are an intelligent, purposeful, competent person, your life will be your message.

What you feel and know when you think of "what I am" is an accurate determination of your present state of consciousness, your true level of awareness. If your present state of consciousness is limited, then many of your best efforts to succeed will fail. You may experience some successes, and you are certain to do so if you persist with right resolve, but total freedom of expression will be curtailed.

Do not let the presence of existing inner conditionings hold you back. Do the best you can, from this moment forward, until you experience inner transformation and are able to creatively function as you are meant to function. Even an occasional minor success will prove to you the truth of these principles. As this occurs your faith will increase, your performance will steadily improve, and you will soon be experiencing the kind of life you are meant to experience.

Our performance is determined by our *beingness*, by our true state of consciousness. From beingness we can learn and do, and by learning and doing, we can accomplish our worthwhile purposes.

Do you remember the burst of confidence you experienced when you first learned to do something well, when you discovered that you could do something which before seemed difficult, if not impossible? With accomplishment arises self-confidence, and from true self-confidence can emerge sometimes almost miraculous performance. Self-confidence here refers to knowledge based on conviction, not pseudo-confidence resulting from temporary "self-image" exercises—although these can be useful to one who is just learning how to function.

You Need Not be Restricted
by Inherited Tendencies

I am now referring to persons who are rational and at least somewhat functional when I declare that one need not be restricted by inherited characteristics or tendencies. If you can think, if you can choose, if you are determined, you can see your worthy dreams come true by accepting and applying these principles.

Every now and again the media will report on people who were born with severe physical limitations, but who did not allow such limitations to prevent them from acquiring an education or doing most ordinary, and sometimes even extraordinary things. Yet there are millions of people who were born with normal abilities and capacities who remain oblivious to life's possibilities, who seem to prefer an almost unconscious relationship to life and who do little or nothing to learn, to improve, or to excel.

The physical body is responsive to the influence of our states of consciousness, our mental states, and our emotional states. It is literally true that we can cause the body to sicken and die, and we can cause the body to be enlivened and healed. Thoughts, attitudes and feelings of optimism, faith and love strengthen the body's immune system and contribute to orderly function. Thoughts, attitudes and feelings of pessimism, despair and resentment produce contrary effects.

Even intelligence, thought by some to be determined

by heredity, can be increased to a considerable degree if the spirit is willing to become more aware and knowledgeable. Our intelligence is measured by our ability to analyze and make correct determinations. Intuitive abilities certainly become more pronounced when we use creative imagination, meditate regularly, and extend ourselves to be more aware of our world, without and within.

As we make demands upon the nervous system it becomes increasingly adapted to processing more refined states of consciousness; in this way the nervous system undergoes any necessary restructuring. It is useful to remember that time is often a factor in the transformation process, as body systems gradually adapt to higher states of consciousness and new ways of performing, so we should be patient as we experiment and grow in the direction of maturity.

With improved function, a more harmonious life style, renewed interest in living and deep meditation, the aging processes of the body are slowed. Conscious, creative people are frequently younger than their calendar years, a fact which has been supported by objective laboratory testing.

Nothing External to You
Has Power Over You

By living in harmony with the rhythms of nature we learn that nature is supportive of us. Really, the external world is not separate from us because the mind and body we use are formed of material substances. Through the use of creative processes we come to know that the universe is a continuum, one organic whole, and that we live and function in an ocean of consciousness. What is considered matter is really consciousness at a slower rate of motion, while mind is consciousness at a higher frequency.

Do not for a moment believe that external circumstances or things have any power over you. Circumstances are subject to change when the causes for them are altered. People will change in their relationship to us when we change our way of looking at the world; individuals who once caused us challenge will move in other circles, no longer aware of us as they go about their rounds.

The problem of addiction, in whatever form, has today become so well known that help groups and clinics do a thriving business. Yet any addiction is but a form of attachment, sometimes obsessive, due to one's lack of awareness of being. Whenever we "need" something—be it a possession, a relationship, recognition, certain foods, alcohol, a drug—to the point of dependency, we are addicted.

We may feel sorry for others who are addicted to food, alcohol or drugs, yet be unaware that we ourselves are addicted in other ways. Perhaps our addiction manifests as possessiveness, greedy acquisition of possessions, habitual negative thinking, indulgence in mood swings, or the maintaining of certain prejudices or unfounded convictions. Our addiction is just as real as is the compulsive eater's, the alcoholic, or the drug abuser. Or perhaps we are addicted to apathy, a self-destructive behavior which is socially acceptable because non-threatening to others, or maybe to being smugly complacent in our egocentric private world.

Again, the underlying cause of addiction is lack of inner awareness as a spiritual being, and lack of meaningful purpose in life. Conscious, functional people are more mature and therefore have fewer addictions. Am I then asserting that addicted people are emotionally immature? Yes, because if they were not they would assume responsibility for their choices and their behavior.

A useful way to handle an addiction is to realize that it is neither good nor bad, but merely an impediment to progress. By assuming this attitude we cease to believe that anything outside of us, or even inside us at the mental and emotional levels, has any independent power to influence the way we choose to experience our inmost reality.

Mental function, emotions, body processes and behavior are responsive to states of consciousness; for this reason we are, as discerning beings, superior to all processes under our direct influence. Once we know the desirable way to think, feel and behave, we can follow through in line with our intentions. Habits, moods, and behavior can be regulated by a gentle act of will—by firm intention. Instead of thinking too much about your personal likes and dislikes, think in terms of what is more useful in the way of thinking, feeling and behaving, and then do what is useful as duty. There may be mild inner resistance to change, but resistance will dissolve in direct proportion to your intentional behavior. Before long you will actually enjoy a life disciplined by reason, and your consciousness will open to a vast realm of limitless possibilities.

It is not uncommon for a person who has been performing unwisely to state, "I don't know why I act like this, because I really know better!" Many people waste their lives acting out predictable dramas, performing according to their conditionings instead of living life in a purposeful and meaningful way.

Emotional immaturity in particular prompts a variety of self-defeating behaviors. A common error is for one to fail to acknowledge that his present mode of relating to others, or his lack of education, is a barrier to achievement. It is common to see persons who have grown up in a lower middle class environment attempting to relate to persons who are more educated in ways which are not at all suitable. They just do not "fit in," and until they learn how to effectively communicate in the circles in which they desire to move they will be at a disadvantage.

Observe people who are functioning as you wish to function, and find out what they know and how they get things done. Acquire all the information you need to do the things you want to do. Lack of formal education is no excuse. Libraries, resource centers, bookstores and other repositories of information are bulging with data which is easily accessible to the person who is willing to learn. I've often observed seminar participants ask trivial questions, not because they are unintelligent, but because they like to hear themselves talk, or they enjoy being in the public eye, or because they are too lazy to read useful material in order to be informed. By all means acquire an appreciation for reading, and learn to comprehend what the author intended to impart. I know there are a few people with reading disabilities, but this is still no excuse for not learning. Such people can usually learn effectively by listening to recorded information, watching video presentations or talking in person with someone who is knowledgeable, while being open and willing to listen and learn.

Even when information is being processed we often miss important points, not because we are not reasonably intelligent, but because at the time we were not able to "hear" certain parts of the message. I'm sure you've had the experience of re-reading a book or listening again to a tape-recorded message or lecture when suddenly, there is a moment of recognition which causes you to think, "Why didn't I see that before?" You didn't see it before because you were not able to see it, or because you didn't want to see it, during that earlier exposure to the material. This is why it is helpful to have dependable source material available—we can refer to it repeatedly until we grasp the entire meaning of the message.

Results Determined by Extreme Effort,
Less Effort, Least Effort and No Effort

According to our state of consciousness and our creative methods, conclusions will be the result of either extreme personal effort, less effort, least effort, or no effort. I'm not talking about a "lazy" person's way to health, wealth and happiness; I'm referring here to how we experience results in relationship to our understanding and function.

The way of extreme effort is the way of achieving results which are directly related to our physical performance. Since we can only do so many things and expend so much energy in a given time frame, we can easily predict results from our efforts. There is certainly nothing wrong with honest work of this nature and many people are presently only suited for such activity. But knowing what you can do in a given period of time, you know beforehand what the results will be from similar effort in the future.

The way of less effort is the way of establishing priorities, making use of labor-saving devices, entering into co-operative ventures with people who share similar goals and purposes, and increasing your effectiveness through these and other possibility-thinking means.

The way of least effort is the way of intelligent use of processes such as creative imagination. By correctly using this method you not only attract to yourself desirable opportunities and circumstances, you also initiate causes in the subtle realm of mind which unfold as events and circumstances. You learn, through practice and experience, that your useful hopes and dreams actually attract the people, resources and circumstances to enable these dreams to be embodied on the screen of space and time.

The way of no effort is the way of grace. When we are inwardly established in the awareness of being, and know that we are in our right place in the cosmic scheme, creative ideas surface, correct responses occur, and the force of evolution expresses through us and around us as a river flows according to the driving force and the conditions of the river bed. We may be actively involved in the performance of duties but we are no longer striving. We are participating in a process which is being directed by the intelligence responsible for the ongoing of creation.

1. Your desires and needs, and your degree of understanding, determine your sphere of action.

2. Success is natural. Failure is due to error.

3. What is true of you is determined by your present state of consciousness and your mental states.

4. By living in harmony with the rhythms of nature we learn that nature is supportive of us.

5. Nothing external to you has power over you.

6. Emotional immaturity prompts self-defeating behavior.

PRACTICAL APPLICATIONS

Here, or in a notebook, write your response to the following questions. Resolve to follow through with constructive actions.

1. What is your highest spiritual aspiration?

a. What are some obstacles to spiritual growth?

b. What will you do to remove these obstacles?

2. Resolve to make full use of your mental capacities.

a. What are your inabilities or shortcomings in the use of your mental abilities? (Included may be poor concentration, clouded intellect, weak memory, laziness, etc.).

b. What will you do to improve the use of your mind?

3. What are your major emotional challenges?

a. What will you do to experience emotional calm?

4. What are your physical challenges?

a. What will you do to experience total health, function and vitality?

5. What are your major challenges in the realm of communication with others, and your world?

a. What will you do to learn to communicate more openly and effectively?

6. What are some of the things you do which prevent you from accomplishing worthy purposes, being successful in ventures, or accepting the fulfillment you deserve?

a. What will you do to eliminate all obstacles to successful function and living ?

7. *A positive action-plan recommendation:* Decide now to order your environment to the best of your ability, eliminating everything that distracts you from your purposes, and adding things which support your purposes. This may include discarding things which clutter your environment and confuse your thinking, rearranging your living or work space, putting your personal affairs in order, writing down plans of action, making decisions about

whether or not your relationships are constructive—anything you can think of to create more order in your life so that your time and energy can be used with greater effectiveness.

Affirm

I am a specialized unit of pure consciousness, made in the image and likeness of God. I am innately endowed with intelligence, determination and decision-making capacities. I make wise choices as I remove from my life all barriers to fulfillment. I rejoice as I participate in life, as a great adventure.

Affirm audibly, quietly, whisper, mentally, rest.

You see, Life is intelligent. Life is all-powerful. And Life is always and everywhere seeking expression. What is more, it is never satisfied. It is constantly seeking greater and fuller expression. The moment a tree stops growing, that moment the Life in it starts seeking elsewhere for means to better express itself. The moment you stop expressing more and more of Life, that moment Life starts looking around for other and better outlets.

— Robert Collier / The Law of the Higher Potential

Finally, brethren, whatsoever things are true, whatsoever things are honest, whatsoever things are just, whatsoever things are pure, whatsoever things are lovely, whatsoever things are of good report; if there be any virtue, and if there be any praise, think on these things.

— The Epistle of Paul the Apostle to the Philippians 4:8

He of whom the sky, the earth, and the atmosphere
Are woven, and the wind, together with all life-breaths,
Him alone know as the one Soul.

— Mundaka Upanishad

CHAPTER THREE

For Lasting Harmony
and Fulfillment, Do These Things

No behavior could be more unwise than to forge ahead with plans and projects while neglecting the basic guidelines which alone can assure complete success.

Through the centuries teachers, prophets, philosophers and sages have repeatedly reminded their listeners to adhere to attitudes and modes of behavior which are universal in their application and which are therefore important for us all to know about and implement. All of the Bibles of the world contain these principles, presented in one way or another, and no person who sincerely intends to experience a harmonious working relationship with the universe can afford to ignore or neglect them.

Love All and Serve All with
Consideration and Respect

This "golden rule" is the perfect one for all relationships. Lived without reservation, it enables us to acknowledge the divinity of all people and to experience harmony with all of nature. *Ahimsa*, harmlessness, means more than non-violence—it means that we are to be devoid of any ill will and free of any urge to injure ourselves, another person, any living creature, or the larger body of nature.

Esoteric teachings assert that one who is established in true love and service will not have any enemies—only friends. He will find that the forces of nature are supportive and that goodness is increasingly evidenced in his life.

Do not try to change people who are content in their ways and who are perhaps working out their freedom in a manner unknown to you. Do not use, manipulate or exploit others for personal advantage. Wish all people well, and with the inner eye of discernment see them as bright, shining beings. In all relationships be willing to quietly set a positive example and to thus encourage the unfoldment of noble qualities in others. Rise above personality differences and prejudiced attitudes. Remember that the best way to help others is to help ourselves to a greater measure of understanding and freedom.

Be Established
in Truthfulness

Be true to yourself, true to the laws of nature, and truthful in your relationships with family, friends and associates. Further, be so settled in the awareness of being that there is no conflict in your mental processes and no emotional confusion. To pretend to be a positive thinker, while at deeper levels remaining insincere or uncommitted, is not being totally truthful. The truth that will "set you free" is the realization of your real nature and your relationship with God and the world. An ancient Vedic scripture declares that one who is anchored in truth consciousness has the ability to cause effects by speaking the creative word. Because there is no conflict at any level, whatever is decreed by such a one must materialize in fact.

*not just
to act...*

Be Completely Honest
and Actualize Integrity

To have integrity is to be whole, complete, and morally virtuous. We are often honest in our dealings with others but dishonest with ourselves. This behavior interferes with the process of transformation leading to wholeness. Be honest in your resolves, honest in your dealings, honest in everything you do.

Circumstances do not cause a person to be dishonest. Circumstances may offer an opportunity for dishonest behavior to be dramatized, but the inclination to be dishonest must already be present in that person. Whatever you need in the way of resources or opportunity can and will flow to you easily and appropriately, in ways which will not diminish others, when you are open to life and honest in your endeavors. Good fortune comes to that person who is honest and who has integrity, while misfortune will be the inevitable result of dishonest behavior, unless repentance and a change of attitude and awareness is experienced.

Wisely Use Your
Energies and Abilities

Unwise and purposeless expenditure of energy depletes our vital forces, weakens the body, impairs mental function, causes emotional unrest and promotes chaos in the environment. On the other hand, the wise use of energies and abilities enlivens the system, invigorates the body, improves mental function, assures emotional peace, and results in predictable success in ventures.

Mental restlessness, unchecked emotionalism, dissipation of all kinds, and unfocused efforts to cause effects weaken our resolve and in no way contribute to wholeness. Cultivation of mental calm and emotional peace, conservation of vital forces, and intelligent endeavor will result in enhanced personal magnetism, superior power of will (rightly used), heightened intellectual ability, awakened intuition and the ability to directly perceive and comprehend the nature of ultimate reality.

Learn to enjoy the silence and be open to the inexhaustible reserves of cosmic force residing in the field of pure consciousness. In these ways vital forces will be transmuted into finer substance to nourish the glands, nervous system and brain, resulting in health and a more spiritually responsive body.

Be in the World but
Not Attached to It

You own nothing. The universe has provided you with everything you need to enjoy life and to be fulfilled. Just as surely as you came into this world you will one day leave it. Remember this as you function in the world without attachment. Renunciation does not mean to have nothing in the way of resources, or to be idle and do nothing; it means that we should be wise in the use of the things of the world but not acquisitive, forever accumulating and possessing to the extent that we mistakenly assume that our security is dependent upon what we own or control.

If you are faithful with small matters you can be trusted with larger ones. Your sphere of influence may become planetary, according to your capacity and destiny, but you are wise to remain aware of the fact that you are but an instrument in the hands of a higher power. You are here to do His will, not your own.

When the substance of the world flows to you, wisely use it and direct the flow for the benefit of others. Know yourself as a citizen of the universe, here to bless the world. You will discover as you do this that the challenge will not

(which is the same as Yours)

(i.e. not your ego's will, which is not)

be how to acquire things or influence, but how to correctly play your role so that only the highest and best results.

See to Purity of Body,
Mind, Motives and Actions

The body can be cleansed and purified through natural means, such as diet and various therapeutic procedures. The mind is more subtle but it, too, can be cleansed of all destructive tendencies, drives and conditionings. Meditate more, use possibility-thinking and creative imagination, cultivate clear thinking, unfold the virtues, and as the months and years pass your mind will become clear so that consciousness filters through it without any distortion.

Examine your motives, your reasons for doing things. Let them be pure so that results are beneficial to you and to others who are involved. With pure motives right actions will be spontaneous. The more you live and express out of your inner awareness the more useful will be your work. The time will come when you will not feel comfortable performing any action unless it is in harmony with nature's laws and, therefore, in harmony with the purpose of the universe. Choose your food, your environment, your associates, your projects—everything—so that your life is lived righteously.

Be Serene and Content
Amidst Constant Change

It is not only possible to be serene and content at all times, it is absolutely necessary that we become so. How is it possible? By turning to the source of all that is and here abiding. The direct way to do this is through meditation and contemplation. With practice, it can be done merely by a shift in attitude and an adjustment in your state of consciousness.

Dispassion is not the same as disinterest. When we are dispassionate, we are not overly emotionally involved in circumstances. We are calm, centered, objective, caring and supportive of constructive results, but without losing our peace of mind or getting off course.

By being serene and content at all times the conditioning process of the mind ceases and the emotional nature is not ruffled. People who think that being creatively interested and intelligently involved means to become drawn into turbulent circumstances are ill-informed. They may have good intentions but their behavior is not wise.

Learn to Appreciate
the Disciplined Life

When we are enlightened we naturally do everything correctly because our actions are directed by a deeper intelligence. Until then we require some self-discipline for the purpose of resisting destructive drives and channeling energies and behavior to constructive ends. Anyone who wrongly assumes that all he has to do to experience fulfillment is to love life, think happy thoughts and follow his whim-guided will will surely one day be confronted with opportunity to deepen his understanding.

Once we know what to do, all we have to do is do it. How deceptively simple that sounds to the ear—but will we follow through? It is so easy to fail in our ventures because of lack of self-discipline! It is so tempting to think that we know better than the experts, better than those who have attained the heights through disciplined behavior. Rigid adherence to rules will not always guarantee results, but it can keep us out of trouble. Being "good" is not alone sufficient to make the difference in our lives, especially since we do not always know what it means to be good. Sometimes we adhere to the letter of the law without comprehending the spirit of it, and sometimes we become so small-minded as a result of concentrating on details that we neglect to expand our awareness.

Study, learn and come to an understanding of what it means to live correctly. Then put what you know into practice. You may discover, as have others before you and as will others after you, that often when you think you "know it all," you really know very little. This is a useful awakening, a new beginning, an opportunity for continued growth and expansion.

Study and Examine
the Processes of Life

Read books written by knowledgeable people. Study the scriptures of your choice. Examine everything you study in the light of intelligence and intuition; that is, contemplate what you are studying until the truth of it is revealed in your mind.

Because knowledge is grounded in consciousness, all knowledge is resident at the soul level. As we ponder the teachings of the seers, and those who have proved the principles of righteous living, we eventually recognize the truth. This is true education, the bringing out from within what has been there always.

Be alert to whatever is occurring about you and learn to see through appearances to causes. Learn to recognize the inner causes of circumstances you experience. As you do you will realize that when a new experience surfaces you will also recall the thought, the wish, the fear, the action of yours which in some way became part of the creative process. Then you will understand that nothing ever happens by chance and that there are no accidents in the universe.

Again and again, return to a study of the basic principles. Do not think that the "new" and the "different" is necessarily better. That which you have been seeking for so long was discovered eons ago by others. When you experience it, it will be new to you but it will be routine for others who have already completed their quest.

Let the Boundaries of
Ego Sense be Dissolved

When the confining boundaries of the ego sense dissolve we experience oneness with the universe, true cosmic consciousness. Egocentric behavior is at the root of all of man's problems and suffering. To function in the world we must have a sense of individuality. If we did not we would only be aware of the unmanifest field of pure consciousness. But we should not be restricted by our sense of individuality. The ideal is to be aware of the ocean of consciousness while, at the same time, being aware that we are assuming our present viewpoint for the purpose of functioning here in this world.

Ego-driven desire causes us to be selfish, fearful, undiscerning and persistent in ventures and relationships which are not useful to higher purposes. Purposeful resolve, directed by intelligence, results in selflessness, courage and wisdom in the performance of duties.

The regular practice of meditation, conscious attention given to becoming increasingly aware of the presence of God at all times, the cheerful performance of duties, daily use of possibility-thinking and creative imagination, and a willingness to live a life of service—these contribute to knowledge and aid in the elimination of egocentric thinking and behavior.

The ten guidelines shared in this chapter, if sincerely adhered to, will assure a firm foundation upon which to build a worthwhile life. You cannot make any major mistakes in judgment or performance if you abide by them.

1. Lived without reservation, the "golden rule" enables us to acknowledge the divinity of all people and to experience harmony with all of nature.

2. To have integrity is to be whole, complete, and virtuous.

3. Know yourself as a citizen of the universe, here to bless the world.

4. Let your motives be pure and results beneficial.

5. Once you know what to do, you have but to do it.

6. Learn to see through appearances, to causes.

PRACTICAL APPLICATIONS

The guidelines in the preceding chapter are the great essentials to observe if we are to live in harmony with the order of the universe.

1. Read the preceding chapter again to see where you need to improve your thinking, attitudes and behavior.

a. In which areas do you need improvement?

b. What will you do to improve?

2. Write your own affirmation, creating one which best suits your need.

_____

_____

_____

_____

_____

_____

_____

NOTES

Open your eyes to the joy of meditation and all darkness will vanish. Worship God in everything and you will find the answers to all problems.

— Paramahansa Yogananda

Let the practitioner of yoga try constantly to concentrate his mind on the Supreme Reality, remaining in solitude and alone, self-controlled, free from desires and longings. . . Having the body positioned in a firm posture, let him make his mind one-pointed; controlling thoughts and senses, let him practice pure contemplation in order to attain inward purity. Holding his body, head and neck erect and still, flowing the attention to the third eye (between the eyebrows) without allowing the eyes to wander, serene and fearless, firm in his vow of self-control, subdued in mind, let him sit, harmonized, his attention flowing to the Transcendental Field which is the Single Reality. The devoted person of controlled mind, ever remaining harmonized, attains to peace, the supreme realization.

— Bhagavad Gita 6:10-15

CHAPTER FOUR
Meditate Daily to Experience
Inner Growth and Spiritual Awareness

The most useful thing you can do to assure inner growth, spiritual awareness and an improved relationship with your world is to meditate, *correctly*, on a regular schedule. If you will do this you will learn to experience the deep silence and rest at the very seat of power and creativity.

I would be remiss in my responsibility to you if I only emphasized in this book those matters which relate to improving your personal circumstances and contributing to your becoming a successful, egocentric materialist. With increased abilities there must be a corresponding unfoldment of soul awareness and an enhanced moral sense. To encourage you, and others, to develop your creative skills and improve your personal performance without nurturing your finer qualities would not only be unfair but would also be contributing to an increase of disharmony in the world.

Meditation is not a mysterious procedure utilized only by mystics and religious enthusiasts. It is a simple, natural and life-enhancing procedure, because it enables one to consciously explore all levels of consciousness and to experience direct perception of reality. Do not confuse meditation with self-hypnosis, auto-conditioning or any other form of mind programming. Meditation is the process of letting the attention be directed to the clear field of consciousness, which clears awareness and leads to a non-mental transcendental experience, the superconscious state.

Superconsciousness is your natural state of awareness when you are conscious and attention is not dominated by thoughts and feelings. We experience unconsciousness when we sleep without dreaming. We relate to the subconscious level when we dream and during the waking state when subconscious influences are present. The ordinary waking state is influenced by drives and tendencies rooted in the unconscious, and by memories which float to the surface of the mind. There are also, during the waking state (and sometimes during sleep), superconscious influences which result in inspiration, clear awareness and a sense of cosmic consciousness. It is during such times that we are most aware of our true nature and our relationship with the universe.

The average person is, for the most part, a victim of his mental conditionings, emotional states, habits and unrealistic beliefs. Because of this he moves through his world driven by impulses which cause him to merely cope, to struggle to survive and to keep on doing this until his life on earth ends. This is the human condition when one is not open to higher possibilities.

Through meditation, contemplation, right resolve and a willingness to learn and apply creative processes you can awaken from "the dream of mortality" and play a conscious role in the world. The process of inner transformation leading to liberation can be fairly easy if you will let go of your self-serving tendencies and enter into a program of reasoned practice which can allow you to awaken to the

↳ = ego - serving
= self - destructive

full realization of your inner capacities. The way will not always be comfortable, because releasing old habits and having the courage to continue in the right direction may go against the conditioned nature, but others have done it and you can do it, too—if you want to do it.

What You Can Expect as
the Result of Meditation

Because of the testimonies of thousands of people, you can be assured that meditation, when regularly and correctly practiced, can be of great benefit to you. If you assert that meditation will not be useful to you and you are unwilling to practice, you have a closed mind and will have to continue through life as you have been doing. You can then read the rest of this book for whatever reason, but you will not derive full benefits from the instruction. Do not waste your time debating the merits of meditation. Do not think that it will not work for you. Do not point to others who may be meditating without seeming results and use that as an excuse for not meditating. The process will be beneficial for anyone who uses it correctly. If persons claim to be meditating and not experiencing positive results, they are not meditating correctly.

Many years ago, when a surge of publicity attended the work of Maharishi Mahesh Yogi and others, many "knowledgeable people" were quoted by the media. Seizing an opportunity to be heard, because meditation was then a popular topic, some said that meditation could lead to mental and emotional problems, disinterest in normal living, and even to "spirit possession." The people who said these things were self-serving and ill-informed. They were not meditators and knew nothing about the process.

Meditation is simply the process of directing one's attention inward, consciously and naturally, so that emotions become settled, the mental field becomes clear, and pure awareness is experienced. This can also occur spontaneously during unexpected moments of transcendence, during which one feels the most fully alive, conscious and serene. What occurs occasionally during spontaneous incidents of transcendence can be experienced intentionally by the meditator who knows how to relax the body, calm the senses and mental activity, and rest in the silence.

When we are overly involved with external and internal concerns, and shifting moods and states of consciousness, there is a strong tendency to become saturated with outer events and inner mental/emotional processes, so that stress accumulates in the nervous system. This contributes to elevation of blood pressure, weakening of the immune system, dysfunction of internal organs, mood swings and mental confusion. Meditation, because it results in stress reduction, contributes to relaxation, strengthening of the immune system, improved function of internal processes, emotional calm and ordered thinking. Therefore, even if you are not presently interested in increased spiritual awareness (but you should be), meditation will be extremely beneficial to you.

When meditation is practiced correctly, because of deep relaxation and emotional and mental calm, superconscious influences can prevail, resulting in an undisturbed flow of fine forces into the mental field, brain, nervous system, and the body itself. Thought processes are ordered, destructive drives and conditionings are weakened, the brain and nervous system are refined, the body is revitalized, intelligence becomes more keen, intuition awakens, insights into the nature and purpose of life are experienced, and a realization of the unity of all life is established. These are just a few of the benefits you can expect as a result of correct meditation practice.

These occurrences will unfold because you are the same as everyone else—you are a spiritual being working through a mind and body, and the procedures which work for others will work for you. What others have experienced you will experience, if you attend to your practices in the right way, with the right attitude and with a surrendered heart.

Meditate Like This
and Prove the Process

Decide now to meditate on a regular schedule for at least six weeks. Don't analyze the process, don't be anxious for results, and don't let your moods determine whether or not you do it—just meditate as duty, because you have agreed to be good to yourself.

There are six progressive stages through which we move when we meditate. Some move through the early stages more rapidly than others. With practice, however, the early stages will unfold quickly and you will easily flow into the silence. Remember, you are not making anything happen—you are *letting* the process unfold.

1. *Relaxation and Inward Turning* —Sit upright in a comfortable posture. Let your hands rest on your thighs, lift your inner gaze, and direct attention to the space between the eyebrows. Do not strain while doing this. Just feel yourself looking *through* this "door" to the inner realms. Inhale and exhale two or three times rather deeply, but don't overdo it. Feel the muscles of your body relax. Be happy and expect the experience to be enjoyable. It will be. Let your breathing rhythm adjust itself, breathing naturally with the diaphragm.

2. *Focusing Attention and Inward Turning* —Let a

word or phrase (or an ideal) float in your mind. If a word is used, such as "God," "peace," "joy," "light," etc., just let it float in the mind every time you exhale. In this way a natural rhythm will be established without effort. Effortlessness is the key to success. I will explain more about this process further on in this chapter.

3. *Perfect Concentration Without Effort* —As you continue, you will soon be concentrating (flowing the attention to one point of focus) naturally.

4. *Now You Are Meditating* —You are no longer relating to thoughts or feelings and memories no longer invade your mind.

5. *Undisturbed Contemplation* —Contemplation is flowing attention to the focus of concentration with the intention of being one with the object of concentration. This oneness results in direct experience, and knowledge, of that which is being contemplated.

6. *Superconsciousness, the Peak Experience* —You are no longer aware of meditating; you are clear, aware, fully conscious and established in being. Rest in this experience for as long as it remains, or as long as you feel inclined to do so. Your attention will then naturally flow back to mind-body-environment awareness and the meditation session is over.

Rest in the meditative calm for a few minutes before involving yourself in personal matters. In this way, superconsciousness will flow into your mind and body more completely and the meditative calm will remain for a duration.

With regular practice, inner serenity will persist even when you are involved with normal activities. You will then be centered, objective, purposeful and able to make wise choices.

In the early stages superconscious influences do not always linger because our attention again reverts to involvement with thought processes, emotional surges and outer concerns. Gradually, however, the nervous system becomes adapted to superconsciousness and its influence remains constant even when we are functioning in routine ways during our waking hours. During sleep, superconscious influences will continue to transform the mind and often result in lucid dreams and occasions of insight and guidance.

The chosen word, phrase or meditation ideal should be one which is comfortable to use. The chosen word or phrase becomes the personal *mantra*, the sound influence which attracts attention and withdraws it from ordinary thought processes and emotional states. Attention becomes involved with whatever attracts it, so by providing an attractive sound influence attention is easily regulated.

Undisciplined attention easily becomes involved with thoughts, moods, sensory experiences and circumstances, causing us to become overly preoccupied with such matters. The easy way to concentrate is to have something attractive to contemplate. We have no problem concentrating when we are fascinated by our own thoughts, strong feelings, interesting relationships or intriguing possibilities. Unless we have learned to become aware subjectively, we tend to be drawn into outer involvements totally, so much so that our consciousness is enmeshed in such matters to the degree that we lose our sense of self-completeness and self-determination.

The word or phrase used during the initial stages of meditation can be one of your own choosing. Perhaps the word "peace" will suffice, or "joy" or "light." If you are religious you may feel comfortable with the word "God" or "Christ" or any word compatible with your religious tradition. A phrase might be, "I am one," with inbreathing and "with the universe" with outbreathing. Let the phrase flow naturally and it will become automatic, without conscious effort. Ponder the meaning of the word or phrase and be willing to let the word or phrase recede from awareness as you become increasingly calm and inwardly clear.

If you do not feel comfortable with a word or phrase (although it will be useful to experiment with them in order to acquire firsthand experience) then merely contemplate an ideal—yourself as expanding in a field a clear awareness . . . .how it would be to experience the dissolving of the ego. . . .what cosmic consciousness would be like. Avoid too much use of imagination during meditation and, when using a word or phrase, do not select one with the intention of programming the mind. The purpose of meditation is to remove attention from the mind altogether, in order to experience superconsciousness.

Meditate at the same time each day if possible. By cultivating this habit you will soon begin to anticipate your meditation session and preparations will occur at deeper levels so that meditation is more effective when actually practiced. Select a time which is best for you. Many find that early in the morning, after restful sleep, is the best time for them. You may have to revise your schedule, retiring earlier at night for this purpose, but it will be worthwhile to do so. Twice a day is a better schedule. The second session can be in the evening, at a convenient time. Allow twenty to thirty minutes for each meditation session, to afford yourself the opportunity to relax and experience full benefits. At other times, shorter meditation sessions can be experienced for the purpose of centering and as preparation for creative work.

The procedure explained here is common to all meditation systems and crosses the boundaries of religious thought. Since it is a natural physiological, psychological and spiritual process, it can be utilized by almost anyone with benefit.

Meditation, in some form, is a necessary prerequisite to using the technique of creative imagination because, as you will learn, it is essential to begin creative endeavors while resting in a state of relaxed awareness.

1. Meditate daily and rest at the seat of power and creativity.

2. Superconsciousness is the natural state of your awareness.

3. You can experience the process of inner transformation leading to liberation of consciousness.

4. When meditation is practiced correctly superconscious influences pervade the mind, brain, nervous system and body.

5. With regular practice of meditation, inner serenity will persist even during waking and sleep states.

6. Let the ego sense dissolve and experience cosmic consciousness.

Note: For a more complete explanation of meditation techniques and procedures read the author's *An Easy Guide to Meditation.* See under "recommended resources" in the final pages of this book.

PRACTICAL APPLICATIONS

Meditation is the most important practice you can include in your daily schedule. Read the preceding chapter again before proceeding.

1. Explain the steps to take in order to meditate effectively.

2. What word, phrase or meditation focus is most suitable for you? (If you are a beginning meditator, don't change the procedure or invent a different one.)

3. What is your daily meditation schedule? When do you meditate, where, and for how long?

4. Meditate as duty, without anxiety for results. Results will unfold naturally. If you are a beginning meditator, meditate on a regular schedule for at least six weeks, to allow yourself the opportunity to experience useful benefits. You will experience benefits sooner, but keep on with your practice. If you are an advanced meditator, deepen your practice.

Affirm

Daily, as I rest in the deep silence of meditation, I experience peace and calm. My body relaxes, emotions settle, mental activity ceases, and I remain centered in the awareness of pure being, pure consciousness.

Take this affirmation into the silence.

For I say unto you, that whoever will say to this mountain, Be removed and be cast into the sea, and shall not doubt in his heart, but shall believe that these things which he says shall come to pass, he shall have whatever he says. Therefore, I say unto you, what things you desire, when you pray, believe that you receive them, and you shall receive them.

— The Gospel According to Saint Mark 11:23, 24

But I have long had the feeling, which this study has matured to conviction, that Fancy and Imagination are not two powers at all, but one. The valid distinction which exists between them lies, not in the materials with which they operate, but in the degree of intensity of the operant power itself. Working at high tension the imaginative energy assimilates and transmutes; keyed low, the same energy aggregates and yokes together those images which at its highest pitch, it merges indissolubly into one.

— John Livingston Lowes / The Road to Xanadu

CHAPTER FIVE
How to Practice the Technique of Creative Imagination

You are now prepared to learn and practice the technique of creative imagination, the process which makes possible the fulfillment of your worthy dreams and the unfoldment of your personal destiny. It is the process used naturally by all creatively successful people. Once you learn the procedure and become proficient in practice, you will also use it naturally, without having to think of it as a formal routine.

Become comfortable with the process and use it often. If you learn it and then neglect to use it you will be missing out on many of life's promises. Should you, at a later time, find that you have been neglecting this basic producedure, return to it to restore harmony to your life. A process, even if valuable, is useless to us if it is not used.

A dictionary definition of *imagination* includes:

The act or power of imagining; formation of mental images or objects not present to the senses, especially of those never perceived in their entirety; hence, mental synthesis of new ideas from elements experienced separately.

During uncontrolled moments we often daydream, and assemble conceptual elements of a theme to form a dream-like mental arena of escape from sense-perceived conditions. Creative imagination is *controlled* mental picturing for specific purposes.

Fanciful daydreaming assembles mental images; intentional imagination gives defined form and exerts a creative force in the direction of outer manifestation. Consciously or unconsciously, we are ever casting forth the enchantments which contribute to the creation of new circumstances or to the modification of existing ones. Our extended world, our environment, is a reflection of our habitual states of consciousness and mental states. Ralph Waldo Emerson, a New England "transcendentalist" of the last century, wrote the following:

Man surrounds himself with the image of himself. Every spirit builds itself a house and beyond its world a heaven. Know then that the world exists for you. For you the phenomenon is perfect. What we are, that only can we see. All that Adam had, all that Caesar could do, you have and can do. Adam called his house heaven and earth. Caesar called his house Rome; you perhaps call yours a cobbler's trade, a hundred acres of land, or a scholar's garret, yet line for line, point for point, your dominion is as great as theirs, though without fine name. Build therefore your own world. As fast as you can conform your life to the pure idea of your mind, that will unfold its great proportion.

Understand and Adhere
to this Procedure

Before you proceed you will have already done your planning and know what your purposes are. Retire to a quiet place where you will not be disturbed.

1. Relax in a state of calm awareness, following meditation or a short period of inward turning. Feel yourself to be a self-complete being. Remain in present-time awareness, with no memories or desires for future occurrences intruding. The ideal is to proceed from a state of inward calm and assurance.

2. In your mind's eye, assemble all of the ingredients necessary to create a finished picture of an ideal condition or event you would like to experience in your world. Envision yourself living in a state or condition you consider to be ideal. Or create in your mind's eye a scene that would imply the fulfillment of your dream.

3. In imagination, reinforced with feeling, establish the realization as a fact, true to all sense perceptions. Experience it as a present reality, not a future-time possibility. The subconscious level of mind obediently accepts as true whatever is offered to it, and it doesn't discriminate between a memory which is the result of an objective happening and an event which is experienced purely subjectively. By imaging, thinking and feeling as though the event or experience desired is a current reality you are able to cause a change in subconscious acceptance, as well as to neutralize any feelings of lack, limitation, failure or inability to function

creatively. You are in fact able to be the person you want to be, allowing you to function from that desired level and experience all things consistent with it.

4. Dissolve into the imagined state, resting for a duration, or even dozing. This will ensure that the memory of the imagined event or circumstance is completely accepted at the subconscious level as true. If you emerge from the practice session before sealing the experience in your consciousness, when you again relate to your environment conflicting "evidence" may flood the mind, adulterating the imaginal state.

We are not deceiving ourselves when we use imagination correctly. We are instead assuming responsibility for how we view our world and contributing to a more ordered sequence of experiences. Through disciplined thinking and feeling we can so regulate internal states that our actions occur spontaneously and appropriately. Also, because of our more open and accepting attitude, we see opportunities which before would have been ignored, and we attract circumstances which can contribute to the fulfillment of desired ends. As we move in the sea of mind substance which is responsive to our mental states, it forms according to the mental patterns we offer to it. Formless substance remains formless until acted upon by a force or impulse. Formed substance also remains formed until acted upon by a force or impulse. The former situation enables us to be active creators, and the latter situation enables us to dissolve or modify circumstances.

Practical Applications
of Creative Imagination

Remember, you can use this procedure to contribute to spiritual unfoldment, to improve your performance at all levels, to replace unwanted circumstances with more desirable ones, to experience healing of any kind, to achieve your worthy goals, accomplish useful things, succeed in endeavors, experience supportive relationships, and to prosper in all ways. All you need is the willingness to enter into the process after you have clearly defined your purpose.

After you have practiced the procedure, live by faith, believing. One practice session, if experienced totally, is sufficient. Several sessions may be required before you are settled in the new state of consciousness and conviction is secure.

If creative ideas surface in your mind and it seems advisable to act on them, do so. If you can clearly see how to initiate positive action to set causes into motion, to create desired ends or to eliminate problems, do so. If you do not know what to do, if a plan of action is not clear to you, remain calm and assured, knowing that expected but unplanned events will unfold to assist you. This is how we live by faith. Even if no sense evidence is present to support our believing, we believe anyway. If the universe is invited to cooperate with us, it must and it will respond.

Do not complain about present challenging circumstances. Do not entertain negative mental conversations and do not engage in negative verbal conversations with family, friends or associates. When you deeply "pray in secret" life will reward you outwardly. This is a never-failing law when we are in harmony with the power that nourishes creation.

If you do not believe it, if you cannot believe it, that is

your own personal problem, and if you want to become creatively effective you will have to change your way of thinking and believing. You cannot think and believe one way and expect circumstances to unfold differently.

When desire and acceptance are in harmony, results are certain. Perhaps you are living a good life to the best of your present ability and desire worthy circumstances and experiences in your life, but at the present time you are unable to feel comfortable in accepting good fortune. Your inability to accept will interfere with your progress. We can experience only according to our capacity. If our capacity is limited, our experiences will likewise be limited. If our capacity is boundless, our possibilities for experience will also be boundless.

With new circumstances come new responsibilities, and with new responsibilities we will need corresponding abilities. We may desire a romantic relationship but be unable as yet to nurture that relationship. We may desire to do great things but be unable as yet to fulfill the responsibilities that accompany such circumstances. We may desire to excel in any number of activities but be unwilling to acquire the education and skills to enable us to succeed. So make your plans according to your capacities, and if end results require of you that you prepare in certain ways, then undergo the necessary training to become competent and proficient in the desired activity.

One common behavior trait of many who are unwilling to change in order to handle new and desirable circumstances is that of sabotaging circumstances before projects have fully matured. Thus, a person may start an argument, or behave irrationally, in order to prevent a relationship from developing. Or he will make mistakes on the job, in order to avoid a desired promotion and new responsibilities; he may even contrive to get fired from the present job.

Many psychosomatic ailments can be traced to an unwillingness to function or be successful. To this end, some people will "get sick," be late for appointments, have "accidents," forget details, eat unwisely, neglect health measures, and so on. These behaviors are indications that the person may have a stronger desire to fail than to succeed.

Another problem is apathy resulting in disinterest and boredom. A functional problem may be present and, if it is, one should see a physician or therapist. But again, it may be that one is resisting the process of living. He will be listless, introverted, and declare that he has no purpose in life, that nothing interests him. Or he may claim that he cannot function without special treatment from others, or without drugs or other substances. Creative imagination can be useful for this kind of personality, for if he will engage in specific and purposeful mental picturing, it will not be long before he begins to evidence interest in life and circumstances will begin to unfold which will further encourage him.

Give your attention to essentials and ignore nonessentials. Don't waste your time and energy debating matters which are not directly involved with your useful purposes. Pay attention to your personal business and leave others to their own. Here is a key to accomplishment: focus your energies through concentrated attention and you will accomplish more in less time, with less effort.

Know *why* you do what you do. If you ask yourself, "What is my purpose in life?" and the response is, "I don't know," then engage in deep thought and contemplation until your major purpose is clearly known to you. If you think, "I'll try this or that; what does it matter, nothing is important anyway," you are childishly immature. Admit it, for at least it will be a moment of total self-honesty.

Here's a true story. I know an attorney who, years ago,

was in a situation common to many men. He was reasonably successful and his family was healthy and happy. When the children reached their teens he and his wife decided to move from their rented house. They decided to buy a larger house in the suburbs, but they did not have enough money to enable them to do it. They used imagination for positive results. Every weekend they drove through areas where they thought they might like to live, and looked at available houses. Finally, they found one which was perfect for them. They took snapshots of the house and imagined themselves furnishing it and living in it. This, in spite of the fact that their financial situation had not improved.

One day a man came into the attorney's office for legal advice. After representing his new client for a few weeks, the attorney's share of a settlement was more than enough to enable him to purchase the house for cash. When he asked his client to tell him who had referred him, the man said, "No one referred me to you. I needed a lawyer and I just walked into the first office I came to."

Were it not for the sake of brevity I could recite scores of instances which have come to my attention, all of which confirm the usefulness of using the technique of creative imagination. When you use it correctly, you will have your own stories to tell, some of them so "miraculous" that many may not be willing to believe them.

I am not recommending that you immediately attempt to walk on water, turn water into wine, see through walls or fly through the air with the greatest of ease. I'm just encouraging you to enter into a rational relationship with life and to be responsible in all of your endeavors. You will discover as you do that you will become privy to the inmost recesses of nature and that life to you will be an open repository of knowledge.

Dramatic physical healings have occurred as a result of

controlled use of creative imagination. Various accounts of such happenings are from time to time published in the popular media, and have been the subject of any number of books. The process used to encourage healing of the body is the same as for accomplishing any other goal. The person in need of healing uses imagination to envision, and to feel and believe, that his body is completely healthy and functional. The body then produces chemical substances which contribute to the healing process.

A widely publicized phenomenon is that known as the placebo effect. A placebo is an inert substance, one that does not cause anything to occur. It is used by physicians to harness the patient's powers of belief.

Tests have shown that a person who has been suffering from pain for which no known medical relief can be found will often experience surprising and dramatic benefits when given a placebo—*if* the patient believes it to be a powerful drug. This does not mean that the patient was not suffering pain from an organic cause, nor does it mean that his belief merely willed the pain away. Blood chemistry tests have shown that what often occurs is that, because of the patient's faith in his doctor and his belief in the usefulness of the "drug," the brain actually produces a substance, similar in effect to morphine, which effectively reduces the pain symptoms. A substance that was not previously present was produced to meet a need—because of the patient's faith!

In many instances of healing resulting from the use of creative imagination reinforced by faith, the people involved have had a strong religious conviction. Their belief in their own ability might have been limited, but their faith in a higher power enabled them to be successful.

Many such former patients have resumed a normal life and have continued to use their creative abilities in positive ways. Some, because of lack of purpose, have become ill again.

What if you are one of those persons who find it difficult to clearly envision possibilities? What if the picture-forming ability of your mind is not developed? There is still a way you can use the process effectively, so don't excuse yourself by affirming limitation. Do this: engage in a controlled mental conversation with a trusted friend or role model, and have that person say, mentioning your name, ". . . . . , I'm so glad to see that you are now spiritually aware (or healthy, happy, successful, etc.)." Then you, in your interior conversation, respond, "Thank you. I feel so good now that I am settled in this new condition." Use your own words, but be sure to have the imagined person say something to affirm your success and fulfillment, and be sure to respond to his or her statement of recognition.

It is popular, from time to time, for some people to teach their followers to contact their "inner guide" and to ask it for guidance, advice and assistance. I don't recommend this because it can lead to fantasy. I'm not saying that it is not possible for us to be in telepathic rapport with knowledgeable persons; I'm saying that if we are not alert we can easily become involved in "mind games" which are not useful. If we falsely believe that we have another source of intelligence within us, we are in error. The ideal is for us to become rational, whole and complete, and this is not possible if we indulge in imaginary conversations with non-existent beings.

The aforementioned procedure of purposely imagining a conversation with a trusted friend is allowable because we know from the outset that we are creating the drama for desired ends and are not self-deceived into believing that the person is actually present.

How to Use Creative Imagination
to Help Others and Your World

We can help other people most effectively by seeing to our own wellness and by providing them with education and encouragement. Our consciousness of wholeness will influence planetary consciousness, and by educating and encouraging others we contribute to their emotional and spiritual growth.

Just as we can be influenced by environmental factors, so can the environment be affected by us. The ideal is to be responsive to environmental influences which are beneficial but impervious to influences which are detrimental. The more centered we are, as the result of deep meditation and purposeful living, the less we are unduly influenced by thoughts, emotions and circumstances in our world. Instead, refined consciousness emanates from us to contribute to harmony in society and nature. If you do nothing more than live a righteous life and remain centered, your presence on earth will make a major difference.

And there are other things we can do to assist ourselves and beneficially influence others. Include some of these practices in your routines. You will become more compassionate, more conscious and more understanding. Even if you work to help others and they do not seem to respond, your efforts are not in vain. You will benefit in the process and you will never know what useful influence you have contributed, even if it is not immediately obvious.

After meditation, when you are clear and centered, inwardly embrace the planet, feel love and goodwill for everyone and thankfulness for the goodness of life. Let the feeling linger even after your practice session is over.

If someone has asked you for prayer assistance, do this: resting in the meditative calm, know that the activity of the Holy Spirit, as the operant influence in the universe, is now active in that person's life, contributing to spiritual awakening, needed transformation, growth and completion. It is not necessary to envision specific results. Just see the person whole, complete, and in his or her right place in the universe. Then, with a thankful heart, release them to their highest good.

What to Do When You Cannot
Clearly Define Final Results
for Yourself

Always, when using the technique of creative imagination to influence the unfoldment of projects, imagine as clearly as you can all desirable end results—leaving yourself open to unplanned good fortune. In this way circumstances will unfold in perfect proportion, not always as specifically as you imagined, and not always limited to your imaginings.

The time will come when you become aware of the fact that you are not always really causing circumstances to unfold but, rather, that you are open to unfolding good and able to select and accept those circumstances which are ideal for your present growth and experience. It is possible to create desired results and still not be fulfilled. This will not occur if you work out of beingness, out of the awareness of self-completeness, for then your experiences will be but interesting and useful episodes which are not expected to add to your awareness of fulfillment.

Do not become complacent with yourself. Just do your best, and be willing to learn and grow. In this way you will be led through successive levels of unfoldment until your destiny in space and time is fulfilled.

1. Creative imagination can make your dreams come true.

2. Use creative imagination to improve your life and bless your world.

3. When desire and acceptance are in harmony, results occur.

4. Healing can occur when imagination is reinforced by faith.

5. Knowledge is grounded in consciousness. You are consciousness; therefore, knowledge is within you.

6. Be prepared for the transition from law to grace.

PRACTICAL APPLICATIONS

Now that you have learned the basics and have been introduced to the practice of meditation, you are ready to proceed with matters relating to the unfoldment and actualization of your potential.

1.   Review the preceding chapter and write the four stages that are experienced when using the technique of creative imagination.

2.   Meditate for at least a few minutes, then enter into the process of creative imagination, observing the procedure to the letter.

a.   If there is an immediate goal or project with which you feel led to work, focus your practice on it.

b.   If you like, use the process for overall purposes. That is, after becoming still and inwardly resting in a state of relaxed awareness, picture yourself as being spiritually fulfilled, mentally competent, emotionally serene, physically healthy and vital, on friendly and supportive terms with everyone and everything in the world, and naturally and easily successful in chosen ventures. Imagine and *believe* to be true everything worthy of you. *Rest in the silence and enjoy the experience.*

3.   After meditation, when you are calm and objective, write a list of your hopes and dreams, for yourself, others

and your world. As you engage in possibility-thinking allow yourself to reach out as far as your imagination will permit you to do so. During this exercise do not think in terms of limitations or restrictions. *All things in harmony with natural law are possible!* Later, you can go over your list and give more attention to what is of immediate interest and importance. Write short-term goals and long-term goals. The achievement of short-term goals will build your confidence and provide experience so that you will learn, by doing, how the creative process works. As you proceed through life some of your goals will change, because you will change. You will become more insightful, more mature, more understanding.

The moment you have conviction about your future, you enter into a cooperative working relationship with cosmic mind and events and circumstances begin to unfold to give your ideal a body. All of the forces of the universe will work with you as you proceed correctly.

Use note pages in this book for this purpose or, better yet, use notebooks which you keep in a private place and refer to from time to time. You will notice that as time passes, many of your hopes and dreams come true without your having done anything other than to believe in them. This proves the creative law in action.

Affirm

Daily I use the technique of creative imagination to enter into a cooperative relationship with the universe. I do so lovingly, sincerely, honestly and with a surrendered heart. I hope for the highest and best, for myself and for all others who may be involved with end results. While doing my best I leave myself open to expected but unplanned good.

I have seen a curious child, who dwelt upon a tract
Of inland ground, applying to his ear
The convolutions of a smooth-lipped shell,
To which, in silence hushed, his very soul
Listened intensely; and his countenance soon
Brightened with joy, for from within were heard
Murmurings, whereby the monitor expressed
Mysterious union with its native sea.
— *William Wordsworth*

We see the truth when we see only the child of God. When we subscribe to this point of view, our outlook on life is transformed. A dark outlook on life is replaced with one of good cheer. Before we know it we begin to see all people in the light of sunshine. What I have been describing is indeed the secret of a happy life. Enemies do not exist when we follow this path.
— *Dr. Masaharu Taniguchi*

CHAPTER SIX
Redeem the Past
with Creative Imagination

You've heard it before. What is past is past. What has happened is history and there is nothing that can be done about it. But is this true? Can effects of past causes be modified so that they no longer influence our lives, or must we remain forever influenced by them?

Time and space must be considered as factors—to understand, to work with, and to no longer limit us as we continue our journey through the relative spheres. Both are manifestations of the creation process and necessary for the unfoldment of nature's inclinations.

Time is the measurement of the unfoldment of events and space is the field in which events occur. Time is observed to occur faster in some dimensions and slower in others, and our own sense of time varies widely. The space we commonly know is not the only space, for there are spaces more subtle and subjective than the average person has yet contemplated.

During moments of transcendence we are literally removed from time and relative circumstances are not observed. In imagination we can move backward and forward through time and we can explore the possibilities of outer space, inner space and perhaps other kinds of space.

All of this may seem a bit complicated for a person who is fixed in time and space by his rigid concepts or by the press of circumstances, yet to contemplate the possibilities of being free to move, in consciousness, in time and space is useful and can be helpful to one who sincerely desires to be a free being. While functioning realistically within the framework of our known world it is possible to assume a new way of looking at it and remove ourselves from influences which are limiting.

How do we arrive at a level of understanding which enables us to see clearly and live freely? There are two ways —the way of contemplation, which enables us to experience subjective understanding, and the way of experience (after knowledge is acquired) which affords us the opportunity to confirm our understanding.

Contemplation is the process of examining a subject, object or concept, with the intention of knowing that which is completely true about it. The truth about matter is that surface appearances are deceiving. We discover that, at deeper levels, ether, gas, water and solids are made possible because of molecules, atoms, subatomic particles, forces, light and consciousness. Seers arrive at this understanding through contemplative meditation. Scientists arrive at this understanding through contemplation and research.

The world in which we live is illusory. It is not an illusion, because it is before us to be examined, but it is not as it appears to be to the senses. Our lack of understanding about the nature of the universe constitutes, for us, the sense of illusion. By not understanding the true nature of the world we remain, to varying degrees, at the mercy of nature's influences—and we even remain victims of prior causes set in motion by ourselves, by others, or by natural forces.

We do not like to be victims. We do not like to remain in bondage, for whatever reason. Our innate urge to be free is frustrated because of a variety of seeming limiting circumstances. What can we do to help ourselves? Is it possible to take a stand and do something about conditions as they are, or should we give up and consider the prospect to be a hopeless one?

Your response will be determined by your present state of consciousness and by your determination, or lack of it. A hero spirit will confront the challenge before him and do his best to put an end to unknowingness and limitation. An immature, partially interested person will exert mild effort to understand the process of life and to improve his circumstances. An apathetic person will merely remain defeated. Yet we all have the same potential—we all contain within us unlimited capacities. The only difference is that some use their abilities and others do not, some are self-determined and others are other-determined. That is, some people decide to do something about their lives and others either cannot do so or refuse to do so, and thus remain at the mercy of past causes and present conditions.

If we are to relate intelligently to the world we must rid ourselves of inner conflicts and conditionings which interfere with optimum function. The major interference is the accumulation of beliefs, concepts, opinions and attitudes which are erroneous. Then, too, there are the mental conditionings which cause us, unless we are very objective, to think, feel and behave in certain ways. These not only interfere with clear perception and the exercise of intelligence, but are also influential—they cause effects. Mental states and mental attitudes cause us to see the world in a distorted way. Our mental states tend to cause corresponding effects and our attitudes cause us to see only a portion of our available world.

Taken together, the accumulation of mental conditionings comprise the karmic condition. The word *karma* simply means "that which causes." Some people like to think that they have no karma. At one level this is true. The being has no karma—the being is bright, clear and perfect. But a being working through a mind has to contend with the mental condition, and if the mental condition is distorted, problems in using the mind will arise.

A major error of many is to assume themselves to be a mind, with its accumulation of conditionings. One will then testify, "I am sick, I am confused, I am unworthy, I am incompetent, because of my karma, because of my present situation." A more realistic attitude is to understand that you are a being with unlimited potential and that even if there are problems which cause the mind to malfunction, or which somewhat restrict your ability to function, these problems can be resolved. The mental field can be cleared and ordered, emotions can be harmonized, the body can be vitalized, and circumstances can be orderly.

How the Mind is Conditioned and What to Do to Be Free

Not all mental conditionings are destructive. Learned routines which we perform without obvious conscious awareness, enabling us to perform basic functions while allowing us to direct attention to other matters, are helpful. Positive habits are helpful. Instinctive good manners and appropriateness are helpful. Attitudes and decisions which will result in constructive ends are useful. What is not useful is the presence of ingrained mental patterns which cause us to perform unwisely, incorrectly or destructively. These should be eradicated.

Let's examine the matter according to how we can be most responsible and effective. The best place to start is in the moment. Do your best to be aware at all times and to perceive without error. Be in open communication with your environment. When you communicate with another person do so accurately and completely. When a person is communicating with you, receive his communication accurately. Be aware in the moment and handle whatever needs to be handled in the moment, without leaving anything to be handled later. I'm not talking here about appointments and scheduling of projects; I'm referring to being in open communication. Drawing wrong conclusions, failing to understand what is happening, falsely assuming something to be so when it is not, and allowing yourself to be emotionally upset are just a few of the ways the mind becomes confused. Experience emotion but don't let your emotional reactions cloud your reason and cause you to behave unwisely.

Many of our sleeping dreams are the result of unresolved conflicts. Not having processed certain information and emotions during waking hours, the subconscious level of the mind does it during dreams. If you examine your dreams you will recognize this to be true. When conflict intensifies in the mind dreams may be erratic, to the point that restful sleep is disturbed. By clearly communicating with your world you will experience restful sleep, during which data processing at the subconscious level is orderly and, at times, you will experience superconsciously induced dreams during which insights occur, problems are solved, and unerring guidance is experienced.

Monitor what you hear, see, feel and think during your waking hours. With training this can be done easily and naturally. When you hear something which is not true you will not believe it. When you see something you will understand the causes behind it. Your emotions will not be unduly disturbed, no matter what occurs. Your thinking will be more orderly and correct. You will learn to think constructively. You will be able to move through a variety of circumstances without their leaving any trace on you. You will become pure-minded, and negative influences will not contaminate your mind or interfere with your purposeful behavior.

Preventing the accumulation of unwanted mental conditionings is the first step in the direction of clearing the mind. You do this by being, thinking, feeling and behaving as you know is best. If you don't always know what is best, emulate those whose lives are proof that they know.

Along with the above, handle inner conditionings as you become aware of them. When you notice that you are thinking incorrectly, because of the influence of a mood, change your thinking and adjust your emotional state. Refuse to be depressed, despondent or apathetic. There are times when you feel inclined to be alone, for the purpose of resting and contemplating. Utilize these times to your advantage, to renew your energy and acquire insight. Learn to discern the difference between restful contemplation and moody self-indulgence.

When you feel impelled to say or do something you know is not useful, resist the impulse or the urge. In this way it will be weakened and eventually neutralized. Channel your energies into positive courses of action and in this way transmute energy and desire to purposeful conclusions. We can master our impulses. We can behave righteously (correctly). We can discipline our senses and remove ourselves from the influences of subsconscious conditionings.

As we proceed, there may be occasions of challenge, of resentment, fear, confusion, pain. You are strong enough and mature enough to handle anything, knowing that when the storms clear you will be the better for having taken your stand.

Use creative imagination to see yourself as you desire to be, as you should be, as you can be. This will extend your awareness and enable you to view life from a higher perspective. See the universe as the field in which you are playing your role in the drama of life. See the past, present and future-as-it-can-be with the inner eye. See yourself as a cosmic-conscious being, no longer confined by any of the restricting tendencies of the mind. Be large-minded instead of small-minded. Be courageous and enthusiastic, not fearful and self-centered. Your positive attitude and your expanded state of consciousness will enable you to succeed.

When memories of past incidents surface in the mind, if they are pleasant memories review them and be thankful for your experiences. If they are unpleasant and bring with them a surge of pain—sorrow, grief, resentment, guilt—then examine them as objectively as you can. Why do you feel sorrow, why do you grieve, why do you feel resentment, why do you feel guilty?

Perhaps your emotional reaction is the result of your having misunderstood prior circumstances. If so, try to understand both causes and effects and release the pain from the memory. Perhaps you were injured intentionally by someone. Perhaps it was not your fault, or perhaps you could have avoided the confrontation, but didn't. Anyway, it happened. What remains is for you to clear the emotional field and be free of the pain. You can do it through understanding, forgiveness and, if necessary, self-forgiveness.

Much of what happens to us occurs because of our state of consciousness. It is not that we intentionally desire to be troubled, but because how we are, in understanding, draws to us those circumstances which correspond to our understanding.

Until we become sufficiently aware to know better, and to make choices, what happens to us is not of our conscious doing. People who are unaware, and who are driven by the urges and tendencies rooted in a conditioned mind, are going to make mistakes. Others have made mistakes in relationship to us, and we have made mistakes which have influenced others, and this is how it is in a world populated by spiritually unaware people.

If others, or circumstances, have traumatized you, be willing to release the pain, release the conditions, and look ahead with optimism. If you have hurt others, or contributed to difficult circumstances, do your best to heal conditions, forgive yourself, and continue your awakening way. Morbid obsession with past events which cannot be changed is destructive. What can be changed are our attitudes, feelings and understanding.

Buried in the depths of the unconscious are tendencies of which we are not always aware. These may surface, sooner or later, and they can be handled with objective ease if we are healthy and functional. Constructive tendencies, if appropriate to one's present life style and purposes, can be allowed expression.

Often we are not happy or purposeful because we have not yet become aware of our major purposes. We may have a "calling," we may be meant to do something which has not yet occurred to us, or which we are aware of but are denying for some reason. We may have aptitudes which have not yet been explored or expressed. Often we do not become aware of these matters until after many years have passed. Then one day our life takes a new direction, and we feel that we are on the right track at last. Proof of this is that all doors open, goals are achieved relatively easily and a sense of lightness and joy pervades our total being.

The world then appears brighter to us, and goodness is apparent everywhere.

Now and then one is confronted with a challenge, with origins in the past, which cannot be easily handled. Here are some suggestions which have been helpful to others.

If you experience pain whenever you recall a past incident, and calm analysis is not sufficient to release the pain of the trauma, *use creative imagination to revise the incident.* I am not suggesting that you suppress the memory, only that you release the pain which attends the memory. Sometimes completely *reliving* the incident, allowing a venting of emotions, will drain energy from the memory so that no further hurt is experienced. The memory is then disarmed and can no longer affect present behavior. This can be a precarious procedure without the assistance of a nurturing therapist, because it is possible to more fully identify with the problem rather than clearing it, or else to become involved with fantasy in response to the urge to escape confrontation or to justify the problem.

Here is a safe do-it-yourself method to use. When bothered by a memory of a past incident which causes emotional hurt, use the technique of creative imagination and *see yourself in alternative circumstances, as you would have* liked circumstances to have been. Relive, in imagination, and with feeling, events in a more desirable way. *In this way redeem the past.*

Your past is nothing more to you than memories and feelings, so use creative imagination to replace unpleasant feelings with pleasant ones. *You will still retain the memory of the past,* but without the trauma.

You may ask, "Would I not be playing a game and merely fooling myself?" You will be enacting a drama, certainly, but you will not be deceiving yourself, for you will only be removing trauma from the subconscious.

A practical thing to do, on a daily basis, is this: whenever you hear or see "evidence" which is contrary to your aims and purposes, use creative imagination to replay the situation or incident and "hear good news." Or, easier yet, dismiss the negative evidence and refuse to dwell on it.

For instance, assume you feel led to do something worthwhile and you know the results will be beneficial to all concerned. But someone you know tells you it can't be done. Instead of accepting that person's verdict as final, use possibility-thinking, creative imagination and intelligent action to accomplish your worthy purposes.

Invite into your personal sphere of activity only those persons who share your dreams and who themselves are possibility-thinkers. Do not intentionally associate with people who are pessimistic and destructive in attitude and behavior.

Superconscious Living and Achievement Makes the Difference

Use the preceding methods from time to time, when you need to, but do not become overly preoccupied with memories of past incidents. Meditate daily to invite superconscious influences into the mind. This is the most purifying experience of all. Then be engaged in useful activities and your achievements will convince you that you are living in the correct way. Synchronize thinking, feeling and behavior so that everything you do is coordinated and purposeful. In this way you will become increasingly responsible and increasingly effective. With successful experience growth is assured, and with growth comes understanding. Our successes do not add to our beingness, but they are evidence of our awareness and competency.

1. Time and space are products of the act of creation.

2. Man's false perception of the world constitutes, for him, his sense of illusion.

3. You are not mind or body—you are pure consciousness.

4. Discover your "calling," your major purpose.

5. Synchronize thinking, feeling and behavior.

6. The good you seek is seeking you.

PRACTICAL APPLICATIONS

Do not be involved in neurotic preoccupation with what has been experienced in the past. Living from *being*, look forward with anticipation. From time to time, when you become aware of mental and emotional conflicts related to past occurrences, redeem the past by calm self-analysis, reason and the use of creative imagination.

1. What childhood traumas have left their mark on you?

a. Clear the trauma by using the procedures here taught. Don't blame anyone or any circumstance for present circumstances. Forgive, release, clear your mind and feelings of all conflict.

2. What experiences of incidents in your adult life have traumatized you?

a. It does not matter whether others were at fault, you were at fault, or that circumstances occurred because of lack of awareness or understanding. Clear the trauma and be free.

b. If there is any "unfinished business" that needs to be taken care of, take care of it and release the past.

3. Remember that conscious, responsible living from now on will dissolve old failure and pain patterns and establish new and more constructive ones in the mind. As you become more able, more functional, more truly successful, you will become more healthy-minded and free.

Prayer

*Lord, make me an instrument of Your
peace. Where there is hatred, let me sow love;
where there is injury, pardon; where there is
doubt, faith; where there is despair, hope;
where there is darkness, light; and where
there is sadness, joy.*

*O divine master, grant that I may not so
much seek to be consoled as to console; to be
understood as to understand; to be loved as to
love. For it is in giving that we receive; it is
in pardoning that we are pardoned; and it is
in dying that we are born to eternal life.*

— Attributed to St. Francis of Assisi

Trust in the Lord, and do good, so shalt thou dwell in the land, and verily thou shalt be fed. Delight thyself also in the Lord; and he shall give thee the desires of thy heart.

— *The Book of Psalms 37: 3, 4*

The best (man) is like water.
Water is good; it benefits all things and does
   not compete with them.
It dwells in (lowly) places that all disdain.
This is why it is so dear to Tao.

To produce things and to rear them,
To produce but not take possession of
   them,
To act, but not to rely on one's own ability,
To lead them, but not to master them—
This is called profound and secret virtue.

— *Lao-tzu*

CHAPTER SEVEN
Prosper in All Ways
and Serve Your World with Love

It is your spiritual duty to prosper—to thrive, to flourish, to be successful in all ways. If you are not prospering you are denying life the opportunity to express through you. The time will come when your sojourn through space and time is over; you will then rest, merged with the ocean of pure consciousness. This will occur when it is destined to occur. Until then your duty is to be as conscious as possible and to prosper so that your world is served unselfishly, with love.

Children should be taught these principles of successful living at an early age. Young adults should be taught these principles and encouraged to embark upon a life of purposeful service. In this way they will be happy, healthy and fulfilled, as well as making a useful contribution to society. People who have not been aware of these principles should be educated and given the opportunity to make their lives worthwhile.

Regardless of one's chosen vocation the information here shared, and the procedures recommended, will guarantee the unfoldment of innate capacities so that success is assured. Almost six billion human beings reside on Planet Earth, and the majority of them need to be informed of the right way to live and of the possibilities available to them.

A natural life, lived in accordance with these principles, is the best foundation to support growth and the fulfillment of personal destiny. One can enjoy family life, business activities, leisure time, occasions of community service —whatever seems best to do—while continuing to study, learn and grow. Within the framework of any circumstantial condition it is possible to begin, and to experience the inner transformation which can result in needed change in circumstances. To deny this is to assert that there are limits to what can occur when one's states of consciousness and mental states are correctly adjusted. There are no external limitations which can resist the aspirations of an awakened soul when vision is clear and the heart is pure.

The entire secret of creative imagination, resulting in the assumption of desired states of consciousness, is that what one *is*, in consciousness (awareness of being), one will experience as perceptions and circumstances.

This is true for every person, regardless of his present condition in life. What each person is experiencing now is entirely the natural result of the state of consciousness he habitually maintains. Rich or poor, healthy or unhealthy, happy or unhappy, free in an open universe or bound by restricting circumstances, the fact remains that every person is now perfectly expressing and experiencing according to his states of consciousness and mental states. This fact of life confirms the experiences of actualized people and offers hope to those in need.

While gratefully accepting support and encouragement from without, it is a mistake to be dependent upon a person, place or circumstance for our well-being. The only guarantee of permanent security and happiness lies in our own ability to remain established in the awareness of who we are in relationship to the universe.

You may say that you do not know how to live this way, that you do not know how the process works. You do know how to live this way because you are doing so now—you are experiencing exactly what you are in understanding and the consciousness of who you are. The law of causation is now being perfectly demonstrated in your life. If you will examine your thoughts, feelings and attitudes, and compare them to your general pattern of circumstances, you will discover that what is occurring in your life is an exact extension of what you are within yourself.

This means that if a change of circumstances is desired, you have but to change your thinking, your attitude and your awareness of who you are. This done, everything else needed to unfold desired ends will naturally occur. It cannot be otherwise, for the law of causation is unyielding, and it is responsive to anyone who will use it.

When thinking of future possibilities think and feel *from* end results, or conclusions, not *of* them. You can think about them and plan for outcomes, but *feel* and *assume* conclusions to be completed. Internal and external movements will occur which will produce and support unfoldments leading to final results. You will not always know how this is done, but it will be done.

If, during the creative process, you think and feel, "I hope it happens," instead of, "It is settled," the creative process will be modified or aborted.

This side of transcendence the possible states of consciousness, and ways of looking at the world, are endless, because of our shifting moods and the constant changes occurring in nature. Therefore, you can choose the states of consciousness you feel to be most useful to your purposes. If you choose to be weak, inept and dependent, you can assume and maintain the attitudes and states of consciousness which will reflect as this condition. If you choose to be strong, competent and prosperous, you can just as easily assume and maintain the attitudes and states of consciousness which are most suitable. From now on, so long as you remember this instruction, you alone determine the kind of life you will experience. Do not blame any past or present circumstance, incident or person for what you are now, or what you can be. I have given you the inner key, the most secret doctrine, and it is your decision as to how you will use it.

Receive from the Source and Give to the Source

From the inexhaustible source, the unmanifest field of consciousness, creation emerges and is sustained. The process is never-ending. It is continuous. Energy is constantly changing form and cosmic forces are molding the circumstances of nature. The ideal for a conscious person is to be so in the flow of life that he understands that everything about him is given from the source and that his responsibility is to give himself to the purposes of the source.

It is easy to know the major purpose of creation. Behold the obvious trend in the direction of growth and completion in nature. Observe the obvious trend in the direction of growth and completion within yourself. Accept all the good life offers you and extend all the good you can to life. This is how we receive from the source and give to the source. A clear understanding of, and participation in, this process is the promise of personal wellness and the fulfillment of destiny.

In all that you do think in terms of serving life. If anything that you do, in thought, word or deed, is merely self-serving, harmful in any way to living things or the body of nature, it is not worthy of you.

Three major tendencies, usually mixed in influence, cause man to behave in obvious ways. An egocentric person will tend to be self-centered and grasping. Egocentricity mixed with <u>altruism</u> results in "<u>doing good</u>" so long as such actions do not overly compromise self-centered purposes. Enlightened understanding results in generosity and full cooperation with the evolutionary movements of the universe. Behave as an enlightened person and make no allowances for failure to do so, for it is the way to freedom.

Give to life from your abundance, which is provided from the source. Love, bless and appreciate others and your world. Let every action, at all levels, be useful to the health and progress of society. When you love, you are loving. When you give, you have it to give. You cannot give what you do not have, and you cannot deplete yourself of what you have. You have everything because it is innate to your consciousness. Do not give as one who bargains with life, thinking that if you give you will receive from outside of yourself. You receive, and you become increasingly conscious of, an increasing flow of knowledge, energy, ability, and things and circumstances required, from the source. What seems to come to you from outside of yourself is really but an expression of what you have within yourself. The key is to *be* a complete person, not to forever work at becoming one.

Now, after having read this book, read it several times more—once a week for three or four weeks, then once a month, at least, for several months. Answer all of the questions, use all of the affirmations, write down all of your hopes and dreams, meditate daily, and be consciously involved with your duties. If you will do these things the creative power of the universe will increasingly find expression through you.

1. It is your spiritual duty to thrive, to flourish, to be successful in all ways.

2. A natural life is the best foundation to support growth.

3. Live out of *being*.

4. The process of creation is continuous.

5. Receive from the source and give to the source.

6. Enlightenment results in generosity and full cooperation with the forces of evolution.

PRACTICAL APPLICATIONS

You now know how to prosper in all ways and serve the world with love. This is your great commission—your personal commitment and the responsibility given you by life itself. Had you not known these things you would not be responsible, but now you know and you are duty-bound to open yourself to all that life requires of you. Do not shirk your duty. Be resolved, be committed, be faithful in the execution of constructive obligations. You are now one of the fortunate ones on Planet Earth. Let love move through you to fulfill worthy purposes.

1. Do you know what it means to prosper? Write what it means to prosper. To prosper means *to thrive, to flourish, to be successful in all ways.* Write this in the space below.

2. Have you come to terms with your world? If you have, then continue along in your awakening way. If you have not, engage in your disciplined practices, study, meditate and come to terms with your world. When your obligations are fulfilled you can leave this world without regret.

3. In what ways are you now prospering (spiritually, mentally, emotionally, physically, in relationships and in ventures)?

a.   What will you do to improve in needed areas?

4.   How are you presently serving in the world?

a.   What other things can you do, and will do?

5.   If you are a young adult now is the time to plan your future and dream great dreams, while being willing to learn and grow.

6.   If you are settled in your mature years, and performing well, continue as you are while being open to growth. If there is need for improvement, what will you do to improve?

7. If you are approaching retirement, what are your plans for these years of opportunity?

8. If your sojourn on Earth is nearing completion, have you cleared the past, made provision for your dependents or heirs, settled your affairs, and come to terms with the process of transition? Now is the time to do so. As you have lived well in this life cycle, you will continue to unfold and awaken to a greater measure of freedom.

9. If you have many years before you, regardless of your calendar years, write creative plans for the next year, for five years, and beyond. Use your notebook to do this.

Affirmation
I rejoice in life! I thrive, I flourish, I am successful and fulfilled in all ways! The prospering power of the universe flows through me, and all around me, showering blessings upon everyone and nurturing the body of nature. I am thankful to be open, conscious, and in tune with the Infinite!

SUPPLEMENT
Straight Answers
to Important Questions

**When I write my plans, hopes and dreams,
should I do so privately or is it all right to share
this exercise with friends?**

Do it privately, because much of what you write will
be extremely personal. As you do this feel that you are in
total harmony with the universe. Especially do not share
your aspirations with persons who may not share your
vision of possibilities. To do so would invite non-useful
discussion and debate which could weaken your resolve or
confuse your mind.

An exception to this is when you are engaged in planning which includes others—your mate, associates or co-
workers—who are understanding and willing to participate
in the creative process. Such a relationship can be a "master
mind" alliance in which you come together on an agreed
upon schedule for the purpose of meditation, possibility-
thinking, planning, group practice of creative imagination
and perhaps project planning. If this is the case be sure
that everyone involved clearly understands the principles

111

and purposes of the meeting and is willing to fully enter into the program.

Explain more about how I can know, when planning the future, that my desires are worthy. I don't want to make any mistakes or interfere with what God has planned for me.

What you are worthy of is the complete unfoldment of your awareness and the unrestricted use of your innate abilities. If your plans are honest, sincere and include the highest and best for yourself and others who might be involved, you are on the right course. When you are calm and objective, and emotions do not interfere with your intuition and reason, your choices will be constructive. You then need not fear that you will be interfering with the unfoldment of God's will for you.

We sometimes have a problem with the ideal of, "Not my will, but Thine be done." When our consciousness is clear, our natural inclinations respond to inner impulses which have origins in the field of pure consciousness. Therefore, what is desired from this level of awareness is in harmony with the rhythms of nature. If we do not assume responsibility for our attitudes and decisions we will remain as we are, in awareness and experience. The conscious, creative approach to living is not a self-centered approach. It is the way of continual expansion of awareness so that we increasingly experience a correct relationship with life.

I am interested in physical healing. What are some practical things I can do to help myself?

Illness is the result of disharmony. A holistic approach to restoring harmony must include spiritual, mental and emotional wellness because of the intimate interactions which occur between levels of awareness and function. If professional assistance is required, seek out a qualified physician who understands the spirit-mind-body relationship and work closely with him or her. Be willing to be self-responsible for your spiritual awareness and for doing everything else needed to clear the condition.

A total approach includes spiritual practices such as prayer and meditation, the exercise of possibility-thinking and creative imagination, behavior modification, useful routines to ensure needed exercise and rest, and attention given to proper nutrition. The ideal diet for most people is a natural vegetarian food plan which includes a balanced selection of foods which can supply essential nutrients.

Meditate regularly and use creative imagination to inwardly "see" and *feel* yourself to be functional and healthy. The healing process will begin and you will be led to the right procedures which can help you meet your needs. If the "will to live," the desire to be healthy and functional in order to live a happy, fulfilled life, is present then a healing will be easier to experience. Many medical doctors, chiropractors and homeopathic physicians are today aware of holistic methods which can contribute to patient health.

Often, an inner realization and conviction can initiate the healing process. Myrtle Fillmore, co-founder of the world-wide movement known as the Unity School of Practical Christianity, was once challenged by a progressive illness. She attended a lecture on one occasion and heard the speaker say, "You are a child of God and did not inherit sickness or limitation!" Mrs. Fillmore experienced inner conviction and before long was healed.

There are often psychological factors which contribute to physical illness. Hopelessness, feeling unloved, feeling alienated from God, resentment, pessimism, guilt, and other inner conflicts can contribute to changes in body chemistry resulting in illness. To be completely healthy and functional it is essential that we learn to experience inner harmony and harmony with the universe.

Is it all right to use creative imagination
to get promoted to a better job when others are
also being considered for the position?

You should not compete with anyone to move into your "right place in life." In a situation where others are involved and only one person can "win," just remain inwardly centered in the awareness of self-completeness, knowing that what is best for you must occur. If you are in a situation where you feel you deserve a promotion or more responsibility, along with the accompanying benefits, perform well and be open to an improvement in circumstances. If the opportunity is not present in your existing situation you will be led to another place of employment, or even be inspired to initiate your own business activities or creative projects.

In any game situation, just be your best and do your best. If you succeed in winning the contest it will be because you were the most capable at the time. If you do not come in first in the competition, if you have done your best, you are still a "winner."

I am romantically attracted to a certain
person. Can I use creative imagination to cause
that person to become interested in me?

You could, but I wouldn't recommend it beyond the point of meeting and getting acquainted to see if the interest is mutual. Nature will then take her course. Do not, ever, manipulate or unduly persuade another person, for any self-serving reason. To do so is to be unfair, unethical and to interfere with the self-determination of another. Of course, many people are impressionable and easily influenced by circumstances in their environment, and they are inclined to let others make choices for them. What is most desirable in any relationship is mature interaction which is best suited to the growth and fulfillment of the participants.

If you desire a romantic relationship, first be a self-complete person, responsible in all ways and able to enjoy a wholesome relationship—not so self-centered that you are a needy person. As a result you will find that the law of attraction brings into your life a mate who is suitable in every way and the relationship will be supportive and growth-enhancing for both of you.

Don't mistake being "in love" with love. Don't assume that every person to whom you are attracted is meant for you. It may be that the mating urge is causing chemical changes in your body, resulting in strong feelings, and fantasy, which interfere with reason and common sense. This is the subject about which many books and plays have been written. When you are sufficiently mature and responsible, an equally mature and responsible person will be there to share your life, if this is what you want.

What about my children and family members? Is it all right to use creative imagination to see them as I would like them to be?

Better yet, use imagination to see them as they can be —see the highest and best for them. With your children, provide them with a complete education, set a positive example, be a responsible parent, and do your best to bring out their innate goodness—without attempting to determine their future after they become adults. If they have been properly educated and nurtured you will not have to be overly concerned about them.

When I speak of complete education I emphasize that

spiritual training be included. Whether this occurs within a religious framework will be a matter of personal choice or tradition. But it is unfair to children to allow them to grow up without having been informed about the nature of consciousness, their spiritual nature, their relationship through mind and body to the world, and the basic procedures as taught in this book concerning goal-setting and responsible living. Even if a child is not overly interested in such matters, or finds it difficult to understand them, the information should be available just the same. It is a spiritual crime to raise children and send them into the world without having prepared them totally.

Of course, a young person who is curious and who wants to learn will educate himself and seek out learning opportunities. But I often wonder how much different society would be today if more children and young adults had been given a proper, complete education.

When I was growing up I read widely, dreamed noble dreams, and sought out learning opportunities, and I still do this. Perhaps you are like this, but many are not—they require encouragement, and that encouragement should be given them.

Many private schools and colleges do emphasize spiritual and ethical values, along with a well-rounded study program. In India, with influence now spreading to other countries, the Sri Satya Sai Baba Institute of Higher Learning is promoting "Education in Human Values," and the Maharishi International University, located in Fairfield, Iowa, in the United States, teaches all courses based on a study and understanding of the unified field, the realm of pure consciousness which is literally "the field of all possibilities."

Loving and supportive communication between husband and wife, and all members of the family unit, ensures harmony, health, and growth. Now and then in a family unit, as in society at large, there will be individuals whose attitudes and behavior present challenge. These have to be worked with, in a caring and responsible way. Just do not falsely assume that you have a right to invade another person's mind, even if you could, and demand that they live exactly as you wish them to. If you are trying too hard to change others it may be that you have a problem with insecurity or a morbid desire to control others. Be self-honest about your motives.

I am a new meditator. Can I meditate with benefit by following the instructions in this book or should I have more personal instruction?

By following the routine given in chapter four you should be able to meditate effectively and with benefit. If you experience any difficulty, personal instruction could be helpful. Be sure, however, that the person who instructs you is an experienced meditator whose own life is exemplary. Be wary of any method which includes mood-changing aids, "newly discovered" special effects, and auto-suggestion procedures. Be very clear about the purpose of meditation. When we meditate we are merely arranging conditions so that we can experience deep relaxation, a clearing of feelings and thought patterns, and easy concentration leading to the peak experience of conscious, undisturbed awareness.

If you experience difficulty meditating, it may be that other aspects of your life are also difficult and challenging. Learn to meditate correctly, and do so on a regular schedule, and you will find that all others aspects of your life are improved.

Are there any additional benefits to be expected as a result of meditating with

a group? And is it possible to elevate world
consciousness as a result of group meditation?

There can be benefits from group meditation if all present practice correctly. Our presence in the group is supportive, not only of our own efforts but of the efforts of others who may need encouragement. It can be useful to meet with friends once a week, or less frequently, for the purpose of deep, silent meditation for an hour or so. People who are more community-minded may want to meditate together more frequently. Be sure, however, that you also meditate privately on a regular schedule, without dependence upon group practice.

Today in many places of business, schools and colleges, group meditation is practiced daily for fifteen to twenty minutes, once or twice a day. Published reports indicate noticeable beneficial results—better relationships, improved performance, greater productivity and, with students, better study habits and higher grades. If you are in a supervisory position and it is acceptable to do so, you might want to conduct a meditation program for those with whom you work or associate. Several minutes of silent meditation will not intrude upon individual religious preferences or practices and can be a worthwhile addition to your environment.

World consciousness is raised (cleansed) to the degree that we are spiritually awake. So your personal spiritual practices and your daily involvement with self-transformation procedures are the most useful ways to assist society in the direction of optimum health. Gathering a small or large group once a month or once a year, for the purpose of meditating for world peace, just isn't going to get the job done. It's not harmful, and may even be helpful in changing attitudes and behavior, but the results are not transformative. However, when individuals or groups meditate deeply, over a sustained duration, beneficial superconscious influences flow into the environment, and this can be helpful.

Don't become frantic in your efforts to transform the world. God's clock of destiny is running on time and the current of evolution is moving to ensure correct conclusions.

I enjoy meditation but I am not always able to easily relax and settle down. What can I do to more easily relax?

First, meditate when possible at the same time each day. By cultivating the meditation habit you will begin to look forward to your practice and internal adjustments will occur. Decide, also, that your meditation time is for the purpose of inward turning and agree to detach yourself from personal concerns and pressing problems.

If you are religious, prayer will help calm your mind and start the meditation process. Think of yourself as a spiritual being preparing to commune with the Oversoul, the omnipresent Spirit. Feel yourself to be entering the silence where only peace, calm, harmony and beingness exist.

You may find that meditating in a special room or place set aside for the purpose is helpful, as this contributes to adjusting the mood so that contemplation is easier.

A practical exercise you can use is alternate nostril breathing. When seated in a comfortable posture, place your hand so that you can close the right nostril. Breathe in easily through the left. . .pause. . .close the left nostril and breathe out easily through the right nostril. Inhale through the right nostril. . .pause. . .exhale through the left nostril. . .pause. . .and continue in this way for a few minutes. You will soon be relaxed and focused. Then let your hands rest on your thighs and proceed with your meditation session.

Breathing in this way affects the flow of nerve force through the nervous system, balancing the flows and inducing mental calm. Brain wave patterns tend to become coherent and concentration is easy.

Do not hold the breath beyond a brief pause between inhalation and exhalation and do not breathe too deeply or too slowly. Just let the process flow naturally. Remember to keep your attention flowing to the space between the eyebrows while you practice this procedure, and feel the meditative process beginning.

When using the technique of creative imagination is it permissible to do so in a reclining position?

Since you will frequently practice creative imagination just after meditating it is best, then, to remain in the upright posture so as not to disturb meditative calm and concentration. At any other time, when you are contemplating and feel inclined to use creative imagination, any relaxed body position will suffice. Reclining in a comfortable chair is agreeable to some because, while it permits deep relaxation, it is not conducive to deep sleep. Also, when reviewing the events of the day and using creative imagination just before sleep at night, it is all right to lie in bed and then go to sleep after the creative work is finished. If you tend to go to sleep easily, you may want to engage in creative imagination processes in a sitting position, then recline and go to sleep.

Other useful times to meditate and to engage in creative imagination are those occasions when you awaken at night for a few minutes. The important thing is to be conscious enough to concentrate effectively and vividly during the first three stages of the creative imagination process.

Does one have to work diligently to clear the subconscious of trauma related

to past perception and experiences, or
can release occur quickly?

This is an individual matter. It is possible to experience instantaneous release, along with insight or sudden spiritual awakening. Conversion experiences are not unknown, during which one is "born anew" so completely that all restrictions related to past events are totally dissolved.

Frequently, however, what happens in such incidents is a major, but not a total release, resulting in the person mistakenly believing that the cleansing is complete, when it is not. Or release may occur, but due to errors in perception and behavior one again accumulates conflicts and trauma.

Once you are functional it can be useful to nightly review the major events of the day, in sequence, coming to terms with everything that has been perceived and experienced and redeeming the day. By doing this there will be fewer unresolved conflicts to be processed at the subconscious level, during dreams, and less chance of taking into sleep problems which could become more deeply ingrained in the subconscious. In this way you can daily "clear your karma" and not have to handle it later.

Can I be influenced or controlled by
someone else who might use creative imagination
or visualization for this purpose?

Until we are fully conscious and self-determined (our decisions and behavior motivated from soul awareness) there is the possibility of being influenced by circumstances in the environment, including attitudes and beliefs in collective human consciousness. We cannot be influenced by the intentions of others if we are not suggestible. Accept the loving thoughts of others on your behalf but do not fear being controlled or manipulated by the thoughts of others who may think they can control you through the power of their "superior" will. You cannot be influenced unless you agree to be influenced. If you believe otherwise you will tend to create, in your own mind, thoughts and attitudes which may reflect as behavior and experience.

If you are informed that someone is trying to influence you by using visualization procedures, bless that person in your own mind and release yourself from fear and concern. Forget the matter and go about your creative business, anchored in the awareness of the presence of God. You have more important things to do with your life than to worry about trivial matters.

Your own beliefs and attitudes determine your experiences. What do you think is worthy of you? What do you think you can experience? What do you think others are worthy of? What do you think they can experience? Your beliefs and attitudes are the windows through which you view your world and what you see is what you can experience. If you can see spiritual awareness, health and function, creativity and success, this is what you will experience. If you see otherwise, it will be done unto you according to your vision of possibilities.

Is it possible to become so involved with these processes that we become "otherworldly" and begin to live in fantasy instead of living a practical life?

Not if you attend to your spiritual practices and practical duties with the right attitude. You will, sooner or later, arrive at the level of understanding and insight where you see relationships between inner causes and outer effects and the relative world may appear to be like a conscious dream. Insist upon being conscious, rational, practical and knowledgeable, and you will be. This way of life is not for escapists, but for those who sincerely desire to live free in an open universe.

If you find that you are becoming too much of a day-dreamer, that your imaginal acts are no longer under your control, do some inner work and be more disciplined.

Napoleon Hill, author of the famous book, *Think and Grow Rich,* among others, once wrote of an incident in his life which relates to this theme. During a phase of his life he experimented daily, using his creative imagination to "meet with select members of his invisible counselors." He would sit alone in a room and imagine that a group of men he most admired were sitting with him. Included were Jesus, Socrates, and other philosophers and men of knowledge and achievement. He would then engage in imaginary "conversation" with them, asking questions and requesting personal advice—and pretended to hear what they would say were they actually present. In this way he was able to assume different viewpoints and have access to areas of his thought processes ordinarily not accessible to him. He found this to be a very useful exercise until, one day, he became aware of the fact that his mental creations were becoming so real that he was beginning to believe they were actually present. He then ceased the practice for a while, until he was able to maintain the desired objectivity.

What must I be willing to sacrifice in order to be the person I am meant to be, and to do the things I want to do?

To *sacrifice* is "to surrender something prized or desired in order to attain or acquire something considered to be of greater worth or value." Whatever is presently preventing you from actualizing your soul capacities and fulfilling your worthy dreams will have to be surrendered. You will have to release all inner restrictions, all nonuseful beliefs and attitudes, and change inappropriate behavior, in order to be the person you are meant to be and thus do the things you should be doing.

It has been observed, however, that most people who are successful in the use of these principles have some spiritual conviction, and many have strong religious feelings even though these are not always clearly defined or expressed in community worship.

Contrary to conclusions drawn by some materially-minded "experts," the religious impulse in man is not due to his need to hold onto something because of his neurotic insecurities. What I refer to as "spiritual aspiration" is innate to the soul, which is our basic beingness. Sooner or later spiritual awakening occurs and an examination of the entire range of consciousness cannot then be avoided.

There are underlying teachings common to all of the world's religions, and there are also underlying spiritual, psychological, moral and behavioral guidelines which are universal and applicable regardless of professed beliefs or station in life. By putting the principles and procedures explained in this book into practice, you are certain to come to appreciate all that is good and useful.

It has been noticed by many that, with improved health and function and an enhanced appreciation for living, a degree of spiritual awareness is also experienced.

The suffering and hardships of many of the people of the world concerns me. What can I do to help improve conditions?

The first thing to do is actualize your own potential and live a free and unrestricted life. While involved in this, open your mind to possibilities about how you might effectively assist others, both near at hand and far away. Use whatever influence you have to interest decision-makers in a positive direction, without losing your peace of mind or emotional balance.

I have known of good-hearted, well-intentioned people becoming so emotionally involved in "righteous causes" that they lost their perspective and therefore their effectiveness. One person who was wealthy and respected became so involved with anti-nuclear projects that he became involved in street demonstrations, to no avail, and lost his credibility with the very people he was trying to influence. Another person became so involved in volunteer work with an organization that she depleted her physical, emotional and financial reserves and had to withdraw for a period of renewal.

Do whatever practical things you can do to help others while, at the same time, maintaining the conviction that all major problems can and will be solved. As the number of people on the planet who think like this begins to increase, useful actions will follow. Remember that even those for whom you feel compassion are experiencing according to their present states of consciousness. I am not asserting that they are consciously responsible for their circumstances, merely that if their consciousness was different, their thoughts would be different and their behavior and circumstances would be different. Planet Earth is rapidly becoming a "global community," one in which we share equal responsibilities. Just as we should be involved in helping members of our immediate community, so we should expand our awareness to include all people everywhere.

Explain more about the right way to give of ourselves in relationship to giving from the source.

Think of your life, everything you are and do, as your service to others and all of nature. Just as our self-improvement endeavors should be multi-leveled, ignoring no aspect of wellness, so our helping endeavors should be multi-level, with all aspects of human wellness considered. Give of your thoughts, actions and resources to assist in personal and world enlightenment through education and spiritual practices, to contribute to the health and stability of individuals and society, and give to cultural activities, without which no society is truly civilized.

If you are presently so involved with personal duties and projects that you have little time to give to other worthy causes, regularly give a portion of your resources so that the money will be well used. Many people enjoy tithing, freely giving ten per cent of their income to organizations, individuals and groups on the front lines performing valuable services. Some who are more affluent give more generously. They report that their participation opens their consciousness to a greater measure of available good and they become better managers of their personal affairs and of their resources. You will be pleasantly surprised to discover how much good can flow through you when you are open to it.

Along with intentional practices and involvements what about the usefulness of having fun now and then?

When we are intentionally involved we have the most fun possible. We should enjoy living, experiencing and learning. Happiness is the natural result of natural and correct living. Some describe the happiness experienced when life is lived from the center of being as "bliss consciousness," which is constant and superior to temporary satisfactions.

A common expression which is often heard is that of spending "quality time" doing things which are life-enhancing. Ideally, all of our time should be quality time;

every moment should be meaningful as we see ever more clearly into the heart of reality.

Do have fun now and then, doing the different, the unusual, things which afford emotional release and the unfoldment of creativity. Throughout nature we observe the necessary cycles of activity and rest. Even our hearts beat in measured cycles of activity and rest. Let your daily schedule include cycles of creative activity and occasions of deep rest, not just during the hours of sleep but also during deep meditation. Schedule periods of recreation—walking, swimming, tennis, golf, bowling, skating, a night at the theater or a concert, a visit to a museum or planetarium, a shopping excursion, browsing at the library or a bookstore—whatever is fun, relaxing and educational.

Cultivate abilities and skills. Play a musical instrument, learn a new language, paint in oils or watercolors, join an investment club, become skilled in the preparation of natural foods, write poetry—let your imagination be your guide. You will not only be happier, you will also improve your overall skills and be a happier, more relaxed person. Your personality will mature and the full capacities of your mind will be explored.

Recommended Resources

If you have found this book of interest you will also enjoy the author's companion book, *An Easy Guide to Meditation*. It explains the correct and natural way to meditate for deep relaxation, stress reduction, emotional calm, ordered thinking, strengthening of the immune system and spiritual unfoldment.

Chapters include: Meditation and the Positive Response - How to Practice Meditation - What Happens When We Meditate - Experiencing Life as It is Meant to Be - Routines for Advanced Meditators - and The World Can Be Blessed Because of Who You Are. The epilogue explains The New Era: Epoch of Great Opportunity and Call to Personal Responsibility. A final essay deals with An Examination of Superconscious States, Transformative Occurrences and Enlightenment.

128 pages, softbound, $3.00 per copy. Obtain *An Easy Guide to Meditation* from your book source or use the address below. Enclose an additional $1.00 for postage and handling costs.

CSA Press, *Publishers*
Box 7, Lake Rabun Road
Lakemont, Georgia 30552

Seminars and Retreats

Special programs are offered at CSA headquarters in the northeast Georgia mountains from spring to autumn. Roy Eugene Davis often speaks in many parts of the United States and in other countries. For information on programs and a current book list contact: Center for Spiritual Awareness, Box 7, Lakemont, Georgia 30552. There is no obligation.